For you shall go out in joy,
    and be led forth in peace;
the mountains and the hills before you
    shall break forth into singing,
and all the trees of the field
    shall clap their hands.

—Isaiah 55:12

We may ignore, but we can nowhere evade,
    the presence of God.
The world is crowded with Him.
He walks everywhere incognito.
And the incognito is not always hard
    to penetrate.
The real labour is to attend.
In fact, to come awake.
Still more, to remain awake.

—C. S. Lewis

AND THE TREES CLAP THEIR HANDS

Faith, Perception, and the New Physics

Virginia Stem Owens

WILLIAM B. EERDMANS PUBLISHING COMPANY
GRAND RAPIDS

Library of Congress Cataloging in Publication Data

Owens, Virginia Stem.
   And the trees clap their hands.

   1. Religion and science—1946-   . 2. Physics—
Religious aspects—Christianity. I. Title.
BL265.P4095 1983   261.5'5   82-21093
ISBN: 0-8028-1949-4

Prologue

FROM the moment of birth, each human creature embarks upon a lifelong task of figuring out the world. Even as he sucks in his first gulp of the world's air, he encounters a creation that constantly threatens to overwhelm his small craft of intelligence with the waves of stimuli that batter his brain in an unremitting storm. How is he ever to make sense of it all? Is there any sense to be made of it, or is there only the chaos of constant random motion? Is the meaning we make of it only a thin membrane we stretch to hold the world, precariously and provisionally, together?

The infant lives in the midst of a riot, a welter of physical stimuli. Yet if he intends to set up housekeeping on this shore where he's been so unaccountably cast up, he must, Crusoe-like, begin to construct some kind of shelter for his consciousness, a structure that will order the raw sensory stimuli.

Physics is one way of figuring out the world. It tries to wrestle down samples of the world long enough to discover what it's made of and how it works. All in all, it's a satisfying method. It gives one a sense of really getting to the root of things. But there are questions that come up in the course of pursuing matter that demand decisions. Where does one begin, for example—or end, for that matter? If one is eventually able to identify the ingredients in the cosmic cake, does that mean the recipe is equal to the reality? These annoyances that accompany figuring out the world are called metaphysics. The decisions these kinds of questions demand may be made offhandedly, desperately, or in a fit of pique. The important point is that they *are* made, and as soon as that happens, the investigator has committed himself, whether he acknowledges it or not, to certain assumptions. There is no physics without a corresponding metaphysics. One cannot even begin without deciding to begin. It is metaphysics that determines the very question about the physical world that an individual or an age allows itself to ask.

The evidence of this indissoluble connection between physics and metaphysics has in fact been documented by contemporary historians of science, who have traced it back at least as far as the pre-Socratic Greeks. Whether a culture has committed itself to a world view that emphasizes isolation, variety, and disjunction or to one that stresses unity, consonance, and correlation shows up not only in its science but also in its politics, economics, art, and spiritual enterprises.

For a good many generations, however, these annoying metaphysical decisions have been made mostly by default, and afterwards deliberately ignored. Their existence as a necessary part of the scientific undertaking has even been denied. Science, full of its intellectual oats and expanding its territory exponentially with new discoveries, grew fretful under the steady demands of its slower-paced partner. It tried to shake itself loose from its inconvenient alliance with metaphysics, like a successful businessman shedding his dowdy wife. The question of what the world "meant" was dismissed as not only irrelevant but impertinent. The only business of physics was to describe whatever was there, not to make judgments about it.

Then, unaccountably and almost with the perfect timing of poetic justice, the world began to dissolve in the hands of the scientists, to run through their fingers like water. The more fiercely they wrestled with the world, the closer they looked at the stuff it was made of, the further it receded from their grasp. No sooner had they concocted one way of describing it than it turned another and unexpected face toward them. The world, it appeared, was made of no-thing at all. Just an ultimately elusive sort of energy. Loren Eiseley has even reported that one poor fellow was driven to wearing snow-shoes day and night so that he wouldn't fall through the insubstantial world. Today physicists continue to invent new names for the myriad "particles" they discover—clever and intriguing names such as "quark" and "strange"—but they hesitate to call them "things." They are more accurately described as necessary parts of a thought process.

For the first time in any of our lifetimes, physics has become flagrantly and self-consciously metaphysical. Ever since matter turned coy with its pursuers, physicists have had to coax it with questions of meaning. Indeed, interpretation is now such an integral part of the new physicists' understanding of the universe that it can no longer be ignored or made a mere philosophical afterthought to the description of the basic structures of being.

For centuries science has tried to operate as though the world and our understanding of it could be kept in two separate compartments. In one compartment were the bare facts; in another were the fairy tales those so inclined made up to explain why the facts were as they were. This included not only religion and poems and legends, but also the remnants of a good many civilizations that had wrecked themselves against the superior solidity of the scientific method.

The new physics, however, can no longer properly recognize such distinctions between kinds of truth. It tells us that, if we can know anything at all about the world, it is that everything is related to everything else. Truth cannot be compartmentalized. The implications of this are yet to be felt by a society that insists science and spirituality are separate disciplines to be pursued in separate facilities so that one may not contaminate the other.

Most of the metaphysics of this movement in science has so far taken a decidedly Eastern tone, as one can tell from the titles of the books published on the subject—*The Tao of Physics*, for example, and *The Dancing Wu Li Masters*. Even Fred Wolf in his award-winning book, *Taking the Quantum Leap*, claims that an understanding of the new physics should change one's life forever, in much the way we expect a religious conversion to alter one's perceptions.

Needless to say, Christians in this country have not exactly found the implications of the new physics a burning issue. Among Protestants, in fact, knowledge of the natural world has never been a high priority, and "natural theology" has been an empty category. They have taken as their touchstone the biblical pronouncement that the flesh availeth nothing, and thus have sought to approach the spirit directly, unmediated by matter. Even the sole mediation of Christ between God and humankind is understood as an entirely spiritual transaction, having nothing to do with matter.

All the natural imagery of Scripture that calls for creation to participate in the praise of its maker has been demoted to the level of mere metaphor and decorative figures of speech, or else seen as unfortunate vestiges of a primitive people's animism. For ever since the age of Newton and the classical laws of physics, civilized folk have agreed that matter is essentially a manipulable machine. No "spirit" or knowledge was observed to inhabit matter, regardless of the psalmist's assertion that the heavens proclaim the glory of God, that the day pours forth speech and the night declares knowledge. And Christians, as creatures of their culture, have been content to bump along with Newtonian laws of motion, adding an occasional vague reference to Einstein and the relativity of time and space.

To be sure, we have continued to beat the dead horse of the Enlightenment, blaming its intellectual errors for the immorality and arrogance of the secularism under which we all stoop today. But at the same time we have been only too eager to profit from the products such a pragmatically based science turns out. We have failed to see that by consuming the fruits of a science that denies the permeation of matter with meaning, we too have acquiesced in a science that leaves the world for dead.

Even the moralistic stewardship-of-the-earth understanding of our relation to the world reinforces this science to some extent. It reduces creation to capital, assets for us to expend as prudent market analysts. Protecting something we call the environment, like the moralistic monitors of society, simply leaves us with the unenviable job of keeping unruly exploiters in line. Thus we are tolerated because we provide a useful balance for society.

At present, however, the scientific community is preparing to line up on entirely different issues. On the one hand are those who see matter as fundamentally dead and dumb, inhabiting an equally dead void of space. Often they are the very ones who are intent on the possibilities of finding extraterrestrial life somewhere, out there, in space. The matter they see right here on earth, of which they themselves are made, they assume follows basic mechanical laws, completely passive under scientific investigation, with no "mind of its own." Any mysterious goings-on observed in it they dismiss as mysticism and folderol.

On the other hand are those scientists who have reason to suspect that matter itself is at some level sentient, informed with knowledge. In other words, that we are living in an at least potentially conscious cosmos.

Those in this second group find themselves unprovided with ways of thinking about such possibilities, except as they discover them in Eastern religions. The Christian tradition, even among Catholics, has almost abandoned the pursuit of God in the world's flesh. Whereas it used to be imperative for theologians to know as much as possible about the nature of matter, physical theories of the universe have become less and less cogent to theology.

Nevertheless, the Christian tradition does have means (buried pretty deep by now, to be sure) to appropriate new ways of figuring out the world. It was the Church, after all, that insisted no model of the universe, neither Galileo's nor Ptolemy's, could ever be equated with its total reality. But an age intent on the pragmatic side of science, on learning how to manipulate the controls of what it perceived as a vast machine, discarded that kind of intellectual rigor. Consequently, over the centuries, the Church, too, has almost forgotten its own concern for precision of thought and purity of science. Presented with a new model of the universe, it finds itself without a means of taking in this fresh, demechanized possibility. It cannot seem to lay its hands on the old treasures of thought it long ago put away as outdated and impractical.

The perceptual merits of the discipline of Zen, however, are readily apparent. The initial encounter with an imported spirituality foreign to one's culture can indeed shock the sensibilities into attending to reality in a new way. But the past, as the new physics itself testifies, is not so easily disposed of. The intellectual traditions and the imagery of the Christian Church are too closely intertwined with science to be torn asunder in such a cavalier fashion.

Yet unless we want to continue with the same religion/science schizophrenia our society has been supporting through the past few centuries, we need to incorporate somehow the fresh data the new physics is offering. This book is an attempt to do that.

Only a full embrace of the Incarnation can open our eyes to its interpenetration of all being, its redemption of the whole cosmos, which is the biblical claim. To see ourselves as separate and distinct from the physical world is our terrible inheritance from the Manichees. Such a heresy leads to the enormous excesses of our current technology.

The task begins with answering one of those annoying questions science thought it had left behind: how important is matter? The Manichean contempt for matter that early infected the Church still plagues it today, and indeed undermines all areas of human endeavor. We continue to imagine that we can exist as disembodied intelligences. The resurrection of the body has only the dimmest possible meaning for us. Such contempt for creation lays the groundwork for an unwitting alliance between religious spiritualizers, whether of the demythologizing or the supposedly literalist school, and a science that would have us believe that matter itself is dead and thus would strip everything "merely" material of significance. Even, ultimately, ourselves.

In a secular society such as ours, devoted to de-sacramentalizing and de-carnating the world, the very concept of "holy" becomes an empty category. Yet this vacuum cannot now be replenished by going back to a dualistic understanding of a "spiritual" world over against a "physical" world. It is not a case of mind over matter because mind *is* matter, and no less hallowed for that. As Owen Barfield has insisted, we can no longer be satisfied with a "religious" truth that fails to implicate matter—and vice versa.

An explication of the new physics that is only discursive, however, fails to give any indication of the urgency, elegance, and richness of the subject. It cannot show how all of life must incandesce and pulsate with this understanding of the universe that is groaning in travail. We live a cosmic drama just by opening our eyes and metabolizing carbohydrates, and it is imperative to engage matter on those terms. Therefore, what follows is no philosophical discussion of propositions, but an attempt to find the flesh from which the propositions were extracted.

I declare that the prophet's figures of trees clapping their hands is a living reality and that Paul's image of living Christ's life is simultaneously symbol and fact. This is the reality of matter we have not dared to dream. To declare this reality one must allow one's own life to flow into this tributary of testimony.

And take upon 's the mystery of things,
As if we were God's spies.

—Shakespeare

Chapter I

My companion and I sit by the window in a coffee shop, watching snowflakes spin and drift to the solid sidewalk, where they dissolve upon a touch. Faces float past outside the glass wall that separates us from the cold; we scrutinize these visages for the several seconds it takes for them to struggle against the wind and pass out of sight again. We are watching the patterns that the snowflakes, drifting and dissolving, and the faces, intent against the wind, make through this slit in the wall and in time. This space and this moment effloresce before our eyes. We drink them in with our coffee and metabolize the vision in our brains, storing up the images from the refracted light as engrams, memories to ponder, perhaps forever. The crystals of ice, the formulations of faces become transmuted through our attention into other chemical structures swimming in our craniums.

Essential information is imprinted on both the faces and the snowflakes. That is why we pay our attention, why we watch so closely. Information essential to what makes up the world floats and drifts past the window. A cross section of the cosmos presents itself for our inspection. Six-sided crystalline frames of ice-stars, a finite shape falling in infinitudes of variations from the leaden sky; the faces, themselves locked within the limitations of their form, yet, like the flakes, never replicated.

And something more. The mystery of things. Something we cannot quite see, any more than we can see the six individual sides of each snowflake or the molecules oscillating within the faces. Something else the flakes and faces struggle against as it batters them, impels them, almost without respite, at each moment and at every turn.

For years my friend and I have both been trying to see this thing like the wind. We observe its effects: the hollows and grooves it has incised across the sheer, reflecting surfaces of faces and into the intricacies of the unresisting snow. But the thing itself eludes our direct vision. Just as the eye of man is made in such a way that it can never behold a bare electron, not even with amplified optical aids, but must rely on the tracks such particles leave behind for any knowledge of their nature, so we can only trace the markings this motion leaves in its wake as it races down sidewalks, down skies, through bloodstreams and brains.

That is why we sit in coffee shops and scan faces as they filter by unawares on the sidewalk. We are collecting, sorting, storing the data. But we do not call ourselves scientists; we cannot make controlled experiments. In life there can never be a control group. There is only what is—or what presents itself, at any given moment, for our perusal. And we, with our own limitations, can only be in one place and one time at any moment. For this reason we call ourselves spies, for we must strike a trail and stick to it. We must catch as catch can, life being no laboratory, spreading our senses wide and drawing them in again to study what we have managed to snare in the wind.

We have several covers, my companion and I, business we appear to be about while we are actually always watching for signs of the invisible prey, which is our primary occupation. He, for example, balances church budgets, counsels divorcées and delinquents, writes sermons. But beneath it all is a constant watchfulness, a taking note. Even as he stands in the pulpit, he sifts the faces of the congregation for those fine grains, no larger than the dust of pollen, that carry the spoor of the trail he's on.

And I sit among them there, internally knitting them up like Madame Defarge, listening, recording, watching, remembering. Softly, softly. The clues one must go on are often small and fleeting. A millimeter's widening of the eye, a faint contraction of the nostrils, a silent exhalation, the slight upward modulation of the voice. To spy out the reality hidden in appearances requires vigilance, perseverance. It takes everything I've got.

Forty years ago it came easy. Absolutely nothing got by me then. Even now a name, a color, an aroma will come back to me from those early years with extraordinary vividness. These first sensations were not the blunted surface impressions made on a dull brain. They went deep; they sunk in. My neurons must have leapt, exploded, gyred, oscillated in constant reciprocation with phenomena.

For the child, newborn, is a natural spy. Only his inherent limitations impede him from consuming all the clues of the universe fitted to his perceiving capacities. Sent here with the mission of finding the meaning buried in matter, of locating the central intelligence, he goes about his business briskly, devouring every detail within his developing grasp. He is devoted to discovery, resists sleep in order to absorb more data. Never again will he seek to unearth the treasure buried in the field with such single-mindedness. He has to learn the world from scratch, but the task seems nothing but a joy. Yet gradually, over time, something goes wrong.

The spy slowly begins to forget his mission. He spends so much time and effort learning the language, adopting the habits and customs, internalizing the thought patterns flawlessly, that somehow, gradually, imperceptibly, he becomes his cover. He forgets what he's about. He goes to school, grows up. He gets a job, collects his pay, buys a house, waters the lawn. He settles down and settles in. He wakes up each morning with the shape of his mission, what brought him here in the first place, grown hazier, like a dream that slides quickly away. He frowns and makes an effort to remember. But the phone rings or the baby cries, and he is distracted for the rest of the day. Perhaps he forms a resolution to remember; still he seems helpless to keep the shape, the color of his mission clear in his mind. Then one morning he wakes up and only yawns. It must be there somewhere, buried in the brain cells, but at least superficially the memory is erased. The spy goes native.

I know that over the years I've grown more skilled at analyzing my information. I sort it, sift it, arrange it in various kaleidoscopic patterns until I come up with something I can actually log as significant. Still, I can't help thinking that if I could only regain that early perspicacity—that sharp sight, that ear for inflection, that scrupulosity of scent—I would indeed be in on some central secret, easily and effortlessly, with no need for laborious analysis.

But living in exile as I do, I must maintain my double existence at all costs. I cannot afford to forget my mission. Forget who you are and you cease to be. You sink down, like the girl in Andersen's fairy tale, beneath the marsh slime into the stifling darkness of a newt-like existence. Blind and barriered.

There are those who will think they have caught me out. They imagine they have discovered my ruse, that I am using something like allegory, casting myself in the role of spy to make a point. But this is not the case. When I say I am a spy I am in earnest. I intend no coy figure of speech. I am playing no literary tricks.

My friend and I do indeed sit by the window in the coffee shop. We watch the faces and the snowflakes melting on the sidewalk with just the intensity I have tried to describe. I consider this spying. All the world rushes by and has no idea what we are about, while bits of the central secret of the universe glint from the sidewalk, glance from the liquid surfaces of water and eyes, beat upon my skin.

I am trying to adjust, as precisely as possible, the focus on this picture of two people sitting at a window. I have falsified nothing in order to make a point—not the setting, not the characters, nothing. This story is not an allegory. I want to tell you what is actually going on here, all around you, instead of the bleared apparition you think you see.

I give every appearance of being only another unit of the populace. I was verified in the last census. Innumerable times on countless forms for employment, taxes, and credit, I have had to list my occupation, my education, the number and age of my children, where I live. I live in a house indistinguishable from thousands of others across the undulating

land. I eat the food, wear the clothes, drive the cars
it produces. Nevertheless, I am an alien. My allegiance lies
elsewhere. I live in a constant state of treason, disguised.

I intrigue daily to keep alive my double existence. The effort required is enormous; the pressure to capitulate, unremitting. One is surrounded by those who already have defected,
who have either forgotten or renounced the mission that
makes them.

The name of this country we all live in is Time. It is my
mission, and that of those who are also implicated in this intrigue, to colonize Time, to salvage what portions we can, to
haunt it with memories of its origins, to subvert the popula-
tion who were all, at one time, spies.

The life of one in such exile is inexpressibly sad. The
Babylonian lament echoes everlastingly: *How shall we sing the
Lord's song in a strange Land? If I forget thee, O Jerusalem, let
my right hand forget her cunning.* The threat that hangs over
the spy in an alien land is not discovery or persecution, but
forgetting Jerusalem, erasing the memories of a distant home,
so that he comes to believe that this bleared Babylon is all
there is, and nothing lies beyond its borders.

We all forget to some degree. It seems impossible to maintain a bright and undimmed vision of the Eternal City in the
wasting atmosphere of Time. The acid rains of despair wash
it, etching away the edges. The image fades, becomes only a
figure of speech. We allow ourselves to be convinced that it is
less than a memory, a mere wish.

I spoke of my early years, when I was fresh on the field.
That, too, was no figure of speech, no clever attempt to
describe childhood. It was a way of escaping Time's perversion of truth, of describing our actual situation here.

Consider these startling bits of information. A newborn
child comes into the world with the apparatus for sight, but
not knowing how to use it. Over a period of a few weeks he
must learn the skill of seeing. Initially, the bright blurs that
strike his retinas have no meaning at all as "things." Yet
despite his limited capacities, his primitive equipment for
dealing with our Time-bound world, he quickly learns to

discern discrete objects. He figures out the fact of three dimensions, that there is more to the world than, literally, meets the eye: that there is another side to all he grasps; that, though invisible, the other side of his ball is round and solid like the side he can see. Most often this knowledge is a delight. He drinks in the world of time and space gladly.

Compare this eager response of the newborn to that of adults, however, or even older children, who through surgical processes are allowed to see for the first time after a life of blindness. They are most often totally disoriented and almost always terrified by their new sight. It takes not months but years of painful training to do so much as distinguish simple shapes. They seem unable to assimilate the visual information that assails them and make sense of it. Far from learning to see easily and naturally as the newborn does, welcoming each new apparition, they are frightened, often to the point of withdrawal, and beg for the bandages to be replaced over their eyes.

How to account for the difference? Obviously, the older surgical patients have gotten used to dealing with the world through their other senses. Any change of a long-embedded habit, especially one so basic, is frequently painful. The agony itself is understandable. But the difference in sheer *ability* to learn to perceive visually remains unexplained. Why do those persons fresh to this world learn to see quickly, effortlessly, and exactly, while those with vastly more sophisticated knowledge of its operation, those who are at home here, those who even have language to aid them, find it next to impossible to see?

The newcomers, of course, still know what they're about. They devour time and space with a voracious appetite. They suck all the world they can hold into their own little sensory vortices and transform it instantly into meaning, for only in the imagination of man does matter become meaning, an even more marvelous transaction than the constant shimmer of matter transmuting into energy and back again. The baby's bath water splashes and drips, the light fractures on its surface, motes dance in the sunbeam—the neurons of the baby's brain map it all ceaselessly, even before a word appears to index the experience.

God spoke being itself into time. He opened his mouth and out tumbled ions, trees, moons. The newcomer still perceives in the same mode. Directly, immediately, the accent and syntax of things being-in-themselves. Who else finds water so funny as a baby in his bath? Who else is so absorbed by its amazing properties to disintegrate and fall back together again? Who else is driven to such an extravagance of tears at the yawning hunger of his interior? Sent here to redeem the time—indeed, the entire cosmos—an infant goes about it with a vengeance.

Years later he won't know what you're talking about. What's so funny about water anyway? He's got a word for it now, and that word "means" water, whereas water itself means nothing at all. He turns aside the questions of his own children as primitive misunderstandings of how the world works. He accepts a cut-rate, impoverished view of himself and all his experience. It all becomes merely—merely matter, merely motion, merely mind, merely water and light and sky. And himself the merest, most trivial part of all. It is hardly his place to go about tearing out raw hunks of time-space, devouring them and converting, contemplating them into meaning. He's no image of God. In fact, his primary occupation, so primary as to be almost unconscious, is to narrow his scope upon the world, to be aware of less and less, to ward off as much sensory experience as possible, and to get whatever he is forced to absorb second-hand, already mediated and masticated for him.

Instead of colonizing Time, instead of becoming a funnel through which Time flows into Eternity, he is himself colonized, devoured by Time. And Time, unredeemed, is death's dominion.

It is this fearful possibility of capitulation that the spy labors under. In the midst of apparent, even practiced, insignificance, he must maintain a sense of the value of his mission. Those around him do not feel this burden, this focusing of the cosmos through the lens of their perception. They yawn, they shrug, they turn away. They have a living to make, they say, and rarely consider the import of those words.

The spy stands among them, indistinguishable and unmarked, no one paying him any mind. Yet against all appearances and the weight of the general inertia, he preserves his infusion of purpose. He knows his mission is urgent.

Incarnation is not an abstraction, not some distant theological principle. It is reality itself. *Res*; things. Accessible to everyone. It starts with fragrant infants' flesh, blood, breath, and tears, and radiates from that single point to include the whole world. Straw, mites, dung steaming in the chill night air, eyes, stars, smells, songs.

It is the spy's purpose to raise this actuality to consciousness, to give a tongue to this truth, not because it will not be truth unless he tells it, but because there is no light in a truth untold, and no joy. In apprehending the flying photons, the electrical charges the world is made of, the spy becomes the film emulsion that traces the signs of their passing. And more than that. In the spy's mind, the passings become pattern. He is an anemometer that scores the will of the wind that creates the world. And only when it whistles through such caverns of comprehension is the movement of the spirit recognized as will. For the spy to fail in this mission is to fall himself into a broth of unapprehended being; to fail is to subject creation to futility.

WHILE in elementary school I stumbled across a series of books that had as their protagonists a pair of twins: one girl, one boy. Each book in the series was set in a different historical or geographical location and the twins were native to the various settings. They were Eskimos, Pilgrims, or Romans as the occasion demanded. I haunted the school library until I had completed the entire series. No doubt the person who wrote the books was trying to teach a little painless history and geography. But I read them in order to discover in their wider experience clues to my own identity. Other explanations of myself—where I came from and what I was doing here—seemed inadequate. There had to be something more to my origins than everyone was letting on. My parents were much too mundane to account for me.

The answer came suddenly one day as I was running through the woods behind our house, charged in that wild way of children who sense that something is about to happen, something that will split the unimaginable sides of the world. I leapt onto a grey stump, my arms flung wide, and balanced there on one foot in one swooping moment of apotheosis. The truth came rushing towards me and coalesced in a single clear notion: my true parents were cave people.

I somehow knew that this was a secret to be kept, especially from my parents. I never suspected them of consciously deceiving me. It was, in fact, they who were deceived and who must be protected from this knowledge. But I was certain that my origin was much too ancient to be limited to them. Cave dwellers were the oldest people I knew about from my time-and-space traveling twins; they were as far back as I could go.

As an adult I learned that such notions form a common fantasy for children. Many besides me, unconvinced by their thoroughly unmythic mothers and fathers, often imagine some further back, more magnificent beings to have brought them forth.

Do not think that my imagination had not been supplied with the figures of Adam and Eve. But they were separated from me by long generations. The list of their descendants did not include my name. I came from my cave parents, however, directly and without chronological intervention. This passionate conviction about my shadowy, potent parentage was my attempt, bereft as I was of adult abstractions, to hold on to a truth that was being torn from me with the years, to remember Jerusalem and my Father, who had spun me into the exile of Time.

I have kept my secret, odd as it is. I don't dismiss it simply because I have learned the word "fantasy." And I search for other secrets, equally odd, equally overlooked. I have not all the time in the world, but all that I can handle. I live it, not with quite the vividness of a newborn, but with a certain ruthlessness. Some who ransack the world for secrets call themselves scientists. Others, with as great a discipline, call themselves Sufis and swamis and Zen masters. Both, by severe training and dedication, have wrestled reality to a standstill long enough to get a good look at it. But I, who lay low and skulk, whose contemplation is done in coffee shops, who takes what falls into the lap, call myself spy. I pick up the secrets discovered by both scientists and spiritualists, stuff them into my pockets, and go on about my business, un-detected and watchful.

Turning and turning in the widening gyre
The falcon cannot hear the falconer;
Things fall apart; the centre cannot hold....
                    —W. B. Yeats

All things were created through him
and for him. He is before all things,
and in him all things hold together.
                    —Epistle to the Colossians

Chapter II

ON my desk is a piece of wood the size of a small loaf of bread. I picked it up on a walk around a lake in the Bridger Wilderness where it had washed up on shore. Somehow it retains the peculiar lightness of driftwood. Even in my hand it feels as if it floats. In some of the crevices made by drying and cracking are embedded white alkaline deposits and even grains of sand and fine gravel. I can tell it was firewood before it was driftwood, since on one of its faces and arching around a knot are dark burns. I picked it up because it had a peculiar golden sheen superimposed upon the charred surface. I kept it and brought it home because of the light and dark marks that told its history, and because of the elliptical patterns on its surface that the growth rings had made. After three years it still retains that hovering gold shimmer that originally caught my eye.

I keep it on the ledge above my desk as a part of the evidence. It contains information essential to my search. It is a part of my files, a clue in the scavenger hunt that is the chief business of my life. When I pick it up and feel the concentric waves of the growth rings under my thumb, it tells me the truth. "Indeed," I say to myself, and am steadied on my pen-point.

Anne Morrow Lindbergh records in one of her journals that she spent a large part of one day staring at a pot of red tulips that seemed to be glowing in that incandescent way tulips have. If she could only stare at them long enough, she felt, she would *know* something. She would be let in on a scrap of the central secret.

As a child I was possessed of a potent, brooding conviction that I have only lately been able to articulate. It is this: all the information necessary to the task of understanding what's going on here ought to, by my calculations, be there, out in the open, available to everyone. Those with eyes to see have only to keep their eyes open. Stare at tulips, drag home bits of wood or rocks to put in the windowsill. Acknowledge the temperature and moisture content of the wind on the cheek. Observe the blood that oozes behind splinters. Register the frequency of the voices of children playing in the dusk. Feel out the world. If one paid close enough attention and collated all the evidence, being careful to forget nothing, to discount not so much as the musty nap on a moth's wing, all the data urgent to the inevitability of life would be there. Being simply the tissue of what is, the given, it is available to everyone. All one has to do is not fall asleep or get distracted.

It made no difference to my theory if one lived on an alkali flat or in the Versailles gardens. The essentials for comprehending life were equally distributed at all times and in all places.

In this I am an unwitting confederate of Anaxagoras, a fifth-century Greek whose one book, *On Natural Science*, sold in the Athens marketplace for a single drachma. And also of David Bohm, a contemporary British physicist whose *Wholeness and the Implicate Order* costs considerably more. According to Anaxagoras, "the seeds of all Things" are present in any part of the physical world, so that "all things contain a portion of everything." And thus to know a part is to know the whole. We identify an individual bit of the world— a carrot or a quartz—by "that of which it contains the most." Whereas Anaxagoras used the organic image of tiny seeds, Bohm is stuck with the hygienic term, the EPR effect. It refers to the fact that a subatomic particle, split off from its mates, somehow "knows" and copies the direction of the spin they will take when the lab experimenter gives them a jolt of current. "All implicates all," says Bohm, vindicating Anaxagoras after 2,400 years.

I carry about in my body, in a single cell, the pattern of the universe. I am pregnant with the cosmos. And in Tasmania, buried in a manioc root, is my body. Select a spot, put your finger down anywhere, and you touch the stars. Pay attention to it, and from your fingerprint, like the rays of an aura photograph, reality radiates, meaning sets out, rippling over the immense ocean of energy until it has fabricated the entire universe.

Gnosticism is still the biggest lie of all. There is no special knowledge squirreled away somewhere from the rest of us. The hiddenness, the mystery, is in plain paradoxical sight. If no one recognizes a messiah or a saint, it's because he's looking for something else—or has his eyes squeezed shut. I knew that all one had to do to sniff out the secrets was to keep his wits about him. Not go dozing off after dinner, sated and sluggish. The exasperation in Jesus' voice as he demanded eyes to see and ears to hear was not lost on me. My eyes were peeled to the quick. Most children's are.

But it doesn't last long. The mooring I had to a mythic parentage was cut, and I drifted loose. Any umbilical attachments I might have had to either my origin or my destiny were thrown overboard. Who can say what treasures of effortless information went to the bottom on that voyage?

Yet what is necessary, what is required to make life inevitable—in the way Bach or the crystal lattice structures are inevitable—is still just sitting there, thrumming and burbling away, but for the most part ignored.

And we, who have lost or blurred our first sight, are faced with the task of developing a second sight. What perhaps came effortlessly the first time around—that initial learning to see—now requires disciplined effort, the sweat of Adam's brow. We must be trained in intelligence, broken to bits. The attention life requires, so natural to an intent and drooling infant, exhausts us. Our brains, bent away from their original purpose, must be wrenched back again, and the stress on the material seems to have weakened it.

Spying is indeed a stressful occupation. The anxiety to get things right is immense. Everything depends on it. The fate of nations, narwhales, nucleoli. Consider the testimony of William Carlos Williams, that most compulsive of cataloguers. Williams' work is full of a desperation to get everything in. His long poem *Paterson* includes even the geological inventory of the New Jersey strata. A doctor and a poet simultaneously, he probed every body he could lay his hands on. Feeling out the universe.

But even he, in the end, did not crack the code. He was only a collector, his extensive files no more than disparate bits of data—crumbs of cosmology, but no loaf. Even his prodigious discipline was insufficient.

Would an electron microscope have helped the good doctor? A Masters and Johnson clinic? A computer terminal linked to the Library of Congress? The Dead Sea Scrolls or the lost golden tablets of Moroni? Would a shred of the Shroud of Turin or the case studies of the clinically dead have supplied that vital bit of information?

No more than a single pot of scarlet tulips or a ridiculously light loaf of driftwood from a lake.

What we all live is life. Reality radiates outward from any point at which consciousness touches it. The drama of the most deprived, the most undeveloped aborigine is as illuminating as Marshall McLuhan's experience.

One picks up what lies at hand. If it is a cloud chamber in a laboratory, well and good. If it is the Cloud of Unknowing, drifting and condensing like mist in the cloistered brain pan, that too is both well and good. To take the given and go with it is the great thing. "Only let everyone lead the life which the Lord has assigned to him and in which God has called him." Prisoner, guard, slave, master, circumcised, uncircumcised. Paul gave them all the same advice. Rich man, poor man, beggarman, thief.

Gnostics, ancient or modern, deny the democratic plenitude of our participation in reality. They think of themselves as spiritual capitalists, controlling the means of production. One does not work out one's own salvation. There is no need to see with one's own eyes or hear with one's own ears. There is no use paying attention; however much you pay will never buy the goods. The real thing is kept in a vault in a starry somewhere.

Spies are the subversives in this scenario, chasing the open air with their free lances. And the dangers are as real as in any espionage. In the television script for John Le Carré's *Tinker, Tailor, Soldier, Spy*, a somewhat unstable Soviet agent named Irena explains to her bewildered British confederate the basis of their vocation: "It's the way we are; we spot things other people miss. We just know how to see." But of Boris, her ineffectual Soviet male counterpart, she adds, "He enjoys showing off too much, so he misses things." Self-indulgence is fatal to seeing as a spy.

I'VE claimed that everything, all the vital information for a comprehension of the cosmos proper to our species, is there before our very eyes. Any old hunk of wood that's withstood the weather will do, any crisp Coryoptera corpse on the windowsill, any flake of flesh fallen like manna from the scalp to the shoulders. Reality radiates from each point of existence as surely as stars.

I had been wordlessly convicted of this as a child, sitting in a cedar tree, making up songs. John S. Bell, a Swiss physicist, theorized upon it in 1964. I remember nothing from my songs, but his statement can be summarized: the basic statistical predictions of quantum theory mean that on both a microscopic and a macroscopic level the spatially separated parts of reality cannot be independent. In other words, nothing, not even laser beams, can lop off snippets of the cosmos and clip them to a line like drying jerky, separate, excised, cloven, disjoined. The cosmos cannot cede itself. The universe is profoundly catholic and recognizes no divorce.

In 1972 Bell's Theorem was experimentally verified at the Lawrence Berkeley Laboratory in California. Discrete parts of the cosmos were shown to be wedded at an essential substratum, the marriage sustained over distances by some force that travels faster than light itself. Or, as John Donne put it in 1611, they "endure not yet a breach, but an expansion." Bell calls this force that connects, and of which time, space, and motion are all forms, "that-which-is." Whether you call it by such a Zennish name or by Donne's "gold to airy thinness beat," the cybernetics is the same: simultaneous communion, co-existent information.

Open the book, point to any page, the message is there. *E pluribus unum* and vice versa.

All intelligence agencies and secret services understand this, too, which is why they go, quite literally, to the ends of the earth. In Timbuktu, Dar es Salaam, Woolwonga, and Waitsap, they recruit newspaper reporters, missionaries, businessmen; doctors, lawyers, Indian chiefs. People who, for whatever reason, travel to odd places. Any little neuron will do as a link in a feedback loop. *Everything* has to do with the price of tea in China. If you don't believe it, watch the market fluctuations of agricultural commodities. The grain trade depends on ballerinas and Afghanistan.

Spies come in rings. Feedback forms loops. Force is a field of infinite symmetry. Intelligence unfurls networks. The field must be covered; operatives must infiltrate every outpost. The circle cannot be broken.

Lepers, whose digital protuberances have lost contact with their central nervous system, who have had their connections cut off, understand this to be their primary danger—not receiving signals. It leads to injury, infection, corruption, amputation. Without ceaseless communication shuttling through the body, the uninformed and uninforming parts are damaged and die. I am the vine; you are the branches. Cut off from me you can do nothing.

There is a map, drawn by Benedictine monks at Ebstorf, Germany, in 1280, that depicts the physical world in a circular configuration. At the north is Christ's head; his feet stretch south and his hands extend east and west.

And spies must see, must skulk and stalk and slink about the labyrinths of this world, inhabiting the arteries, clinging to the cilia, immersed in the mucus linings. For a spy is the true contemplative of the Western world. Meditation in motion. Keeping out of the way, unobserved, but antsy and unable to keep still. Tracking, scanning.

"I am impressed with the fact that the greatest thing a human soul ever does is to see something and tell what it saw in a plain way," said Emerson. "Hundreds of people can talk for one who can see. To see clearly is poetry, philosophy, and religion all in one." Jesus went scrabbling over the Judean hillsides looking for a few eyes that could see.

There was enough stuff in the woods near my home to have lasted me for a lifetime of seeing. I knew I could sit in a certain cedar tree, listening to the wind sawing and stressing its limbs, and I would know in time how the world's heart beats. My own interior would become a map of unerring information. I would be the universe knowing itself.

Needless to say, I am not writing this from the cedar tree. I only have a piece of driftwood on my windowsill now. I know a great many things, but not how the world's heart beats. My interior maps all too faithfully the distortions it has spent time reflecting. If the universe is depending on me to know itself, it remains ignorant and dumb to its own destiny. Unlike Emily Dickinson, this soul has not selected her own society.

But the cedar tree is still there. Along with the sweet gum and pines and dogwood and redbud. My failure has not destroyed them, although the collective failure of my species has destroyed many like them.

"Everyone should remain in the state in which he was called." I'm not particularly pleased with the state in which I am called at present. It's not what I would have chosen for myself. The suburban bluegrass is turning brown as the ground freezes. Chain links outline the false premises of each citizen's property. My neighbor's Early American metal storage shed fails to hide the overturned garbage cans in the back alley. Like Chesterton, I daily pose for myself the problem of the universe knowing itself in the suburbs: "the problem of how men could be made to realize the wonder and splendor of being alive, in environments which their own daily criticism treated as dead-alive, and which their imagination had left for dead." The very names of such places reveal the betrayal of every child who was ever coaxed down out of his tree: Nottingham Woods, Big Sky Estates, Vista Grande.

And what am I doing here, in a place some contractor named Buffalo Ridge, instead of up a cedar tree?

Like Tolkien, my life lies in circumstances. His biographer makes apologies for his garage made over into an office, for his electric fireplace full of imitation coals. "The places where he lived were not really chosen by him at all: they were simply the places where, for a number of reasons, he found himself." The imagination that housed Lothlorien led the life that God had assigned to him, and in which God had called him, even submitting to life in the Oxford suburb.

Thoreau carried out his investigations by Walden Pond and in the Maine woods. He drew the easy assignment. Truth hounded his steps—there was no escaping it. I know. I remember how it rises up, surrounding and towering in its substantial reality. But the society the soul does not select, dead-alive and abandoned by the imagination of man—that is the territory of the spy. Where is the that-which-is, the force that connects, that keeps Buffalo Ridge from spinning off into the void, down some black hole that serves as a drain for cosmic effluvium?

Outside the plate-glass window of yet another coffee shop, an elevated boy, plastic and barefoot, stands poised like an acolyte, holding a plastic hamburger aloft. An armada of clouds, shipping tons of snow, moves ponderously southward. Cars wander somnambulantly around the supermarket parking lot. Let everyone lead the life the Lord has assigned to him. Conspire consciousness in the midst of death.

I can't go back and sing in the cedar tree. Not yet. The truth of life among plastic icons and scabrous asphalt has to be known. I am the crippled, groaning universe knowing itself.

*There will be a revival of Christianity
when it becomes impossible
to write a popular manual of science
without referring to the incarnation
of the Word.*

—Owen Barfield

Chapter III

I went to school at a time when science seemed simple. Supplied by the taxpayers with microscopes and Bunsen burners, we watched cells divide and phosphorus effervesce just as the books promised they would. The microscopes and the Bunsen burners were necessary because books by themselves were held to be insufficient sources of knowledge. The current educational philosophy said that seeing with our own eyes was an unassailable part of the rites initiating every adolescent American into that bedrock faith, that religious commitment to science that the age, spurred on by Sputnik, demanded.

As I said, science seemed simple then, at least as it was taught in the public schools. Observation was its keystone. Set up the experiment, stand back, watch it, record it. We had implicit faith in our eyeballs. Even when we had to rely on optical extensions of our own fleshy apparatus—microscopes or telescopes or other mechanisms for measuring, such as graphing indicators geared to record temperature or wind velocity—it was our observation of these records that we, in our innocence, trusted.

It was, of course, a point of honor not to interfere in the experiment. The standing back was essential to the process of observation. In fact, the entire respectability of the scientific method rested on this detachment of the observer—and for good reason. We take it for granted now, but scientists had fought hard for several centuries to maintain the integrity of the inductive method of reasoning, the harvesting of observed data from which general principles may be drawn.

Until the time of Galileo, both physics and astronomy were studied deductively. There was a set of eternal "laws" governing nature by which all physical phenomena were to be explained. Seeing had very little to do with believing. Even

Copernicus undertook the task of unraveling the retrograde motion of the planets not because he had stumbled across some new bit of information previously overlooked, but because he found the Ptolemaic epicycles that had always been used to explain this motion to be clumsy and unattractive. He was certain that whatever law governed the paths of the planets, it would be much more appealing in its simplicity than the tangle of Ptolemy's epicycles. At that time there was no possibility of making a definitive experiment that could "prove" that either the earth or the sun was the center of the cosmos. The eventual acceptance of the Copernican theory was based solely on aesthetics: its simplicity and economy of constructs made it superior to Ptolemy's theory.

Andreas Osiander, the Lutheran clergyman responsible for the publication of Copernicus' work, wrote in its preface,

> [An astronomer] must conceive and devise, since he cannot in any way attain to the true causes, such hypotheses as, being assumed, enable the motions to be calculated correctly from the principles of geometry, for the future as well as for the past. . . . Now when from time to time there are offered for one and the same motion different hypotheses (as eccentricity and an epicycle for the sun's motion), the astronomer will accept above all others the one which is the easiest to grasp. The philosopher will perhaps rather seek the semblance of the truth. But neither of them will understand or state anything certain, unless it has been divinely revealed to him.

Elsewhere in the preface, Osiander praised Copernicus' "huge treasure of very skillful observations." But observation itself was regarded at the time as the impetus for the development of the new hypothesis of a heliocentric universe, not as any kind of proof of the way things actually were. Indeed, Osiander proposed that Copernicus' new theory stand alongside Ptolemy's ancient one, which would continue to be studied and used.

Clearly, the notion of "progress" in science, the superseding of one theory by another, was not yet a part of the sixteenth century's understanding. Theoretical structures of the universe were not disposable to them. Instead of perceiving each new model as ousting the old in some kind of scientific junta, they thought of science more in terms of a museum of the mind where one considered the attributes of each theory on its own merits, much as we house the paintings of modern abstractionists alongside Egyptian stone carvings. The notion of "progress" would have smacked of a crude opportunism, a certain tawdry commercial tone that would have jeopardized the integrity of the scientist. The contemplation of truth, so far as it can be got at by the human mind, was their aim. They acknowledged from the outset the limitations of mere appearances. "So far as hypotheses are concerned," concluded Osiander, "let no one expect anything certain from astronomy, which cannot furnish it, lest he accept as the truth ideas conceived for another purpose. . . ."

Is this merely the quaint reluctance of an early Renaissance clergyman to find finality in any truth except revealed truth, his own special bailiwick? Was this high-handedness with hypotheses only the last exhausted gasp of the Middle Ages while a fresh infusion of intellectual life was being prepared in the Enlightenment? If so, science is suffering a relapse into medievalism today.

In the meantime, Galileo found that first fateful device that would permit the human eye to probe the heavens. Perhaps it was the telescope itself that first gave science the bravado to reverse the direction in which knowledge flowed. Before, it had always begun with general principles, with laws which could then be applied to particular instances. Now it started by gathering "specimens," by looking first at specific occurrences, sorting them all out, and then propounding a principle. Actually, there was nothing before Galileo that we would recognize as "science" today. He was the first to work inductively, gathering scraps of data from the very heavens themselves, sucking in the stars through the tube of his telescope. In fact, "data" as we use the word first began its service in his century.

Was the telescope an extension of Galileo, or was he an extension of this light-bending peephole on the stars? Did Galileo create what we know as the scientific method, or did the telescope give us an exaggerated sense of the infallibility of our observations? Today we hesitate before answering such a question. We waver between the man and the mechanism precisely because we have had so much firsthand experience of our perceptions being altered, modified, even falsified by the sensory extensions electronically supplied to us. Despite the tide of information inundating us about politics, economics, even the weather, who would feel confident proclaiming the "real" truth, the final word on the stability of Central American governments, the root of inflation, whether we are headed for an Ice Age or a swamping of the coastlines?

Still, the scientific method has, for several centuries now, been built on stacking up observations and then sorting them into suitable hypotheses. Doing science in any other way is unthinkable to us. But what did thinkers, those with the talent and leisure to try to figure out the world, do before the advent of Galileo and the elevation of the inductive method?

Scientific popularizers have made much of Galileo's battle with the Church. She is always cast as brutishly incapable of dislodging this human-haunted planet from the cosmic center. As a matter of fact, the Church was indeed willing that Galileo should teach Copernicanism as a hypothesis, which was the very status accorded to Ptolemaic astronomy. What the Church denied was that a hypothesis, any hypothesis (which is, after all, only an intellectually conceived model), could be identical with ultimate truth. Any model might prove helpful to the understanding of reality. But a blueprint is not a building any more than a statistical chart contains all the information about a society. At best, models represent their originals. As Owen Barfield has put it, what was at stake was not a new theory of nature but a new nature of theory. When scientists began to take their models for the real thing, the Church brought the weight of her authority against their intellectual presumption. Whether she was ill-advised to do so, or even morally right, is not our concern here. In the arena of mental discipline, she was undeniably more rigorous than her opponents.

Not everyone fell so completely in love with the inductive method at first sight, as Galileo did. The astronomer had a young contemporary, Rene Descartes, who saw a problem inherent in the method. Induction always depends on data gathered by the senses, which are notoriously deceptive. Furthermore, how is one ever sure that there does not remain out there some other overlooked instance that would throw the calculations into confusion? Descartes did not simply doubt the ultimate accuracy of models constructed to explain celestial or terrestrial behavior; he doubted the very existence of the heavens and earth. Whereas the intellectual tradition of the Western world from the pre-Socratic Greeks to the medieval scholastics had at least assumed some valuable correspondence between cosmic models and the nature of reality, Descartes dismissed all the models, from Plato's harmonic spheres to Copernicus' sun-center, as awkward, bungling contrivances based on illusion. Any kind of theory that started from observation or experiment was doomed to a kind of dream status, because observation depended on the senses, and the senses could be deceived. Indeed, they were most often a distraction from the pure process of reason. For Descartes, seeing had nothing to do with believing. In fact, seeing, clouded as it is by circumstances and contingencies, could only falsify reality. Only the activity cloistered within the brain pan could be trusted. All the flimsy phenomenal world could tear like wet tissue paper at a touch: "Although experience would make us see the contrary," Descartes wrote, "we would nevertheless be obliged to accord more faith to our reason than to our senses."

If the Copernican revolution toppled the earth from its center in the cosmos and replaced it with the sun, Descartes went further, snuffing out the sun itself in favor of the dark, eyeless intellect. Cartesian physics, based on deductive reasoning alone, has not stood up well, although Descartes' contributions to mathematics were considerable. But his philosophical gnosticism, his negation of the senses, was not affected one whit by his failure in physics. Ironically, Cartesian philosophy has provided modern science with what its irascible founder most sought to destroy—an image, one of man as an abstracted intelligence, a detached thinking machine, fighting clear of the vicissitudes of physicality. The theatrical trappings of science visually convey the unexamined assumptions it has inherited from Descartes: the spotless white lab coats worn like vestments, the ivory tower of intellectual isolation, and that perfectly imagined gnostic haven, the ceramic-surfaced sterile laboratory. The medieval thinker kept a skull on his cluttered table as a *memento mori*. Our scientists live inside the skull's smooth white surfaces.

Thus modern science, at least up until the first part of the twentieth century, was a hybrid of these two unlikely parents. On the one hand there was a thorough-going commitment to observation and to representations taken for reality itself; on the other hand was an unquestioned acceptance of intelligence that functioned reliably only in a detached, abstracted mode. And what effect did the combining of these contraries have on human perception? Just this. Scientific seeing was different from ordinary seeing. Seeing could henceforth lead to believing only if done from a distance, if the viewer removed himself by an act of imagination from the same temporal world his object inhabited, if he became above it all, disembodied, static, invulnerable.

As extreme as his position may seem to the ordinary, mundane sensualist, Descartes found an heir he would have been proud of in Werner Heisenberg, another mathematician. At the age of seventeen, he was reading Plato and serving with the German troops that suppressed the revolutionary movements that followed World War I. His early love for classical languages was supplanted, however, by a passion for numbers. Mathematicians tend to be early bloomers; he was only twenty-four when he developed the essentials of what was to be his Nobel prize-winning theory about elementary particles, one he described not in words but in matrix algebra. Yet despite his insistence on austerity of description, Heisenberg was also an admittedly intuitive scientist: "I must not start from detail," he said, "but from a feeling I have about the way things should be."

Of course, Heisenberg was not working with any such massive objects as suns and stars, but with essentially invisible particles of matter. If Galileo needed a telescope to discover that the Milky Way was actually a clabbered conglomerate of individual stars, at least he had had the experience of observing, unaided and firsthand, the phenomena of our own sun and the larger or nearer stars. The word "star" had meaning to him as a description of everyday experience. Heisenberg, however, worked at the other end of the scale, beyond even the aid of optical microscopes. No one, he pointed out, has ever actually *seen* an electron. We can invent mechanisms that track the dispersal patterns of subatomic particles when they are bombarded with high-energy waves, but that is not the same as "seeing," even with a telescope or a microscope. Therefore, he argued, we cannot conceptualize or form adequate mental images of the processes that go on inside an atom. All such pictures would necessarily depend on analogies formed upon everyday experience. Thus atoms have misleadingly been compared to billiard balls, planetary systems—even, at one point, to plum pudding.

The tug of war that developed among physicists over whether matter was best described in terms of particles or in terms of waves made Heisenberg especially impatient. He insisted that both light and matter are "single entities" and that their true nature is only obscured by trying to describe them as one or the other. Once again, language has trapped us inside a framework that science had superseded, just as the pre-Copernican world had been trapped by descriptions of "sunrises" and "sunsets." Thus phenomena that by their very nature are beyond our powers of observation must be described in a language that dispenses with all questions of shape, color, texture, and taste. And only math, he claimed, takes no account of the deluding senses.

If Heisenberg was determined to eschew language in science, his colleague, Paul Dirac, almost gave it up altogether, even in his daily life. This first propounder of the theory of antimatter was both reclusive and extremely uncommunicative. Like Heisenberg, he was leery of using models and pictures to describe quantum mechanics, although he found himself having to descend to that level repeatedly in order to make clear to others how antiparticles work. He called the universal balance between positive and negative charges "symmetry," a word we can understand only by visual analogy.

Dirac certainly was another heir of Descartes. When he developed his theory of antimatter, he did so by employing a process of pure reason with no experimental evidence. In his Nobel-prize acceptance speech he asserted, as Descartes had done, the primacy of theory over evidence. And he later went further, claiming that if observation did not seem to support the theory, that was certainly no reason for abandoning it; there was probably some flaw in the observations that would eventually be revealed.

He insisted on the importance of constructing a "beautiful theory"—that from one who had warned against models and pictures. "It is more important to have beauty in one's equations than to have them fit experiment," he insisted. When asked how one recognized "beauty" in a scientific theory, he replied, echoing Heisenberg, that the individual scientist can feel it. "Just like beauty in a picture or beauty in music. You can't describe it, it's something—. And if you don't feel it, you just have to accept that you're not susceptible to it."

Well, well, well. Have we finally come full circle with science? From the immutable laws of the ancient and medieval worlds through a brief flirtation with evidence and observation and back again to "beautiful" theories that shrug off the pitiful data supplied by experiments if they fail to suit the taste of the scientist? Has a new crop of aesthetical physicists saved us from a crass, soulless scientism? Have they foresworn the mundane vision of molecular billiard balls for a mystical one of ineffable beauty?

But we're not to the end of the story yet. For there is another branch to this tree of knowledge, a grafting of quintessential modernity. And the graft is set into the stock, again, by Heisenbergian mathematics.

When Heisenberg articulated his uncertainty principle in 1927, he knew that the very name would lend itself to philosophical interpretations scarcely more reassuring than Descartes' own fundamental doubt of everything except his individual thought processes. Heisenberg strove to keep its implications confined to the subatomic world of quantum mechanics. But from his own hometown of Munich came a force that threw the world into such disarray that uncertainty found itself proclaimed in every quarter—physics, politics, morality, literature, religion.

This was not the first time that politics and physics have mirrored one another. There has always been a correlation between the perceived state of matter and the prevailing political ideal. At times when the material world has been believed to be continuous, social unity has been favored, just as fragmented, particulate pictures of the physical realm have gone hand in hand with individualism. But since the revelations of the depth of man's depravity in World War II, and the consequent confusion of the relation of a citizen to his society, science has seemed unable to commit itself to either a universe of continuous reality or one of disparate, colliding bits. It is still stuck in the middle, unable to choose between particles and waves, and impotent to create a new image of physical reality for us. Are we one or are we many? Or is there a new vision, a fresh way of seeing that can free us from where we hang between two worlds?

Whatever the answer, the clockwork image of classical Newtonian physics was gutted by Heisenberg's uncertainty principle. Newton and his followers had developed the mythology—no more provable than the Resurrection—that if the precise mass, position, and speed of every atom in the universe could be calculated at any one moment, then one could predict the future and predicate the past of all matter by applying the laws governing the mechanism of motion. The great clock of the universe told the time for everything with regularity and certainty. Cause and effect, the tick and the tock, went on predictably and reassuringly.

But then matter began to be described in terms of waves, a more organic, less mechanical image. The tidy packages we had learned to call atoms, which had bounced about according to forecast, fell open and acted in strange, unprepared-for ways. The fact was, as Heisenberg insisted in his unremitting manner, that no wave motion which can be located precisely in space can also be measured simultaneously for velocity. Not only that, but the very act of "observing" on a subatomic level, done by aiming a beam of high-energy rays at target particles, necessarily stirs them up unnaturally and distorts what *would* have been going on in that particular portion of space had it been left to itself. Uncertainty crept into the scientific method itself: can one clump of matter really observe with anything resembling accuracy the nature of another clump of matter? Even supposing we were Cartesian disembodied spirits watching the world from some empyreal height, our measuring devices, all our apparatus for observation are themselves material and exert their own forces upon the experiment.

So here we are. Cartesian doubt underscored by that sinking principle of uncertainty.

How are we to go on with any part of the human enterprise that requires what we have so loosely called knowing? What is true in physics must be equally true in other disciplines of the mind: psychology, economics, history, biology, meteorology. Either there will always be some hidden, undiscoverable variable inherent in the very act of observing, or there is a certain amount of unaccountable random lawlessness at the bottom of things. Either way, indeterminacy mocks the mind and all its eyes. Is it worthwhile even keeping our eyes open? In an admittedly flawed method, is the considerable effort that observation demands worth it?

Anyone who's staked his life on staying awake wants an answer to this question. Particle physics and quantum mechanics may seem an esoteric study more than once removed from the kind of reality that each of us wrestles down day by day. Perhaps we can afford to ignore such specialized subjects as these. But can we afford to ignore our own experience? The struggle to keep one's eyes open, of staying awake, of transcribing in the memory the record of one's own individual life—is there any point to it? Is seeing through a glass darkly any better than not seeing at all? Why should I strain my eyes to catch a glimpse of the wind?

We all ask the same questions, from the haruspex of ancient Sumer to the operators of high-energy accelerators in California and Geneva. Where are we, anyway? And what's going on here? Is anything—not to mention anybody—home?

Should we "accord more faith to our reason than to our senses"? Are all those pictures we've put together, painstakingly collected over millennia and pasted in our scrapbook of shared consciousness, no more than the imprint of our own interiors, a sketch of our brain structure? Will one picture serve as well as another so long as the calculations come out right? Would I be wise to give up my lifelong efforts at espionage, of seeking out the broad-daylight secrets of this world, and instead pull the blinds, close my eyes, and crawl into my skull?

What is the world made of, made of? A good number of physicists have given up trying to answer this question that has always been the central business of their work. The elusive electron, impossible to trace as an individual unit of matter, has caused them to shift the very nature of their investigation. They are now willing to settle for averages. Speculation is now *en masse*. One aims a cathode-ray gun and shoots a whole flurry of charges at a target. Unable to follow a single electron, the calculator simply averages where they all turn up. So actuality is abandoned for probability. Only the statistical electron is considered. The actual electron and its behavior is given up as a literally lost cause.

Consider another instance of the abandonment of actuality by physicists. They can work out the mathematics, for example, for the average rate at which atomic nuclei decay. But when they try to determine *when* the next alpha particle will break off or *which* alpha particle it will be, the mathematics is not equal to the test.

This averaging happens on a variety of levels, of course, not just in the seemingly surreal world of the subatomic. Suicide rates for different countries, age groups, and economic brackets can be statistically predicted with a degree of accuracy. But who will next turn his hand against himself, or precisely when or where he will do so, is impossible to predict. Likewise with divorce, car sales, twin births.

This abandonment of the "actual," an individual entity and its progress through different states, is seen in more areas than just physics, sociology, and economics. The calculus of probability dominates more and more of our lives. Politics, markets, morality, travel, medicine, allotment of resources, education, agriculture—all are statistically averaged in order to assess their significance. The track of an actual, individual alpha particle, citizen, dollar, disease, holiday, load of coal, book, or bushel of wheat is no longer worth the effort of tracing. Only the multiplication of unseen, unnoticed actuals into a lump that is then divided by the number of its members is worth the trouble of attention. That is why Americans have 2.3 children per family. That is the calculus of probability. But such a figure describes no one's experience. Small wonder, then, that there is a conceptual crisis in the sciences. Statistics have only a tenuous and subordinate relationship to what we experience as reality.

Opting for the "calculus of probability" and denying the importance of the actual means shifting the whole focus of science. Instead of seeking the true nature of matter, scientists are soon happy to have enough mathematics to manipulate *whatever* is there in a predictable, and sometimes profitable, manner. The ability to predict, one of the criteria for judging hypotheses, applies then only to masses, not to actual instances.

Here we can borrow an analogy from Owen Barfield. There is a kind of knowledge acquired by a clever boy who knows nothing about the principle on which an internal combustion engine works, and yet who manages to figure out the correct operation of all the switches, knobs, and levers in order to drive an automobile. But it is quite different from the kind of knowledge possessed by someone who has studied the internal combustion engine and the construction of automobiles, even though he may never have driven a car himself.

At least until recently, science concerned itself with the latter kind of knowledge. Galileo with his telescope would no more have harnessed the revolutions of the planets for his own purposes than Heraclitus would have dammed up his continually flowing stream of reality that is ever-changing.

But technology has gradually become substituted for science in our cultural consciousness. Technology is the "dashboard" kind of knowledge, a superficial grasp of reality that allows us to "operate" the physical world. Certainly the muddling of these distinctions began as far back as Francis Bacon, who insisted that *scientia* "is that which enables us to make nature do our bidding." Bacon maintained quite frankly that science was valuable not because of its dogged pursuit of the nature of reality, not because of the models it provided for the contemplation of truth, but because of the power it gave us over nature. And most of Bacon's heirs have settled for operating the machine in lieu of comprehending the cosmos.

Most—but not all. In 1961 David Bohm and Maurice Pryce, both British physicists, had a discussion on BBC radio in which Bohm expressed his dissatisfaction over experimental results that relied only on the averaged effect of electrons. He insisted that to know anything about the substance of physical reality, experimenters must trace an actual electron, follow a particular particle. Pryce, on the other hand, found this a niggling sort of objection, one worthy only of a "philosopher." " 'Actuality,' " he protested, "is a kind of dirty word that one must avoid in physics."

For J. S. Bell's "that-which-is" Pryce would substitute "that-which-can-be-quantitatively-averaged." Whether or not there *is* any that-which-is to average is quite literally immaterial to him. Particularity is of no intrinsic value. Only the abstraction of averages is important.

IN 1959 I left home and went to college eight hundred miles away. I no longer jumped on stumps for joy at the reality rushing toward me; I had learned better than to postulate other parents than the ones I had documents for.

But life always longs for more of itself. And what life I had hoarded suddenly swelled and grew turgid with the scent and crackling spine of each new textbook, with every fresh, staring sheet of paper, with first French conjugations. It was all coming back to me, the wonder of the world and its immense possibilities.

It was not only schoolwork that aroused this hunger. I was as ravenous for sensation as any infant. The sheer physicality of life swamped my senses. I remember with terrible clarity the irises blooming that spring, the smell of the damp, darkened loam through which their spears thrust, the tender fringed flesh of the petals. To inhale the mingled scents was like sexual surrender, a melting, an inexplicable weeping.

In early summer I had a midday class across town. I went along sidewalks shaded by elms arching over white frame houses. At the back steps hydrangeas bloomed blue from the dishwater the housewife splashed over them. Through the open kitchen windows came the sounds of a spoon scraping the side of a pan, water rushing from a tap, a bowl set down brusquely on a table. The large noon meal of the Southern working class was being laid out.

These sounds, inevitably familiar but transfigured like a sacrament, dilated the world. My own life quickened as it approached the invisible life marrowed within those walls. My senses swam with the richness of it all: the warm, amniotic air, the common human substance sustained so effortlessly. The woman inside was intent on serving her dinner, a dew of sweat around her hairline and above her lip, her cotton housedress soft and limp with pastel flowers. Her husband in his khakis, already seated at the kitchen table, picked up his fork. I knew I had caught it, locked it in the chemical engrams of memory: the real thing.

And in the evenings I would walk, sometimes along the same streets, when the lights were on indoors and the windows open to catch whatever coolness came with the dark. Someone crosses a room, rattles a newspaper. The rooms are lit up like a stage setting against the dark theater of the night, and the people inside are as unconscious of any audience as actors pretend to be. It is all so beautiful, so beguiling. The sweet, deft scorings of actuality on memory.

How could one ever consent to feed on the thin gruel of statistics after such a summer?

The thing itself, whether splintered electron or housewife with hydrangea, is the way I choose to come at the world.

Descartes' distrust of phenomena, the modern acquiescence to averages, the calculus of probability—all steadily lost ground that year. Incalculable, I found, was not synonymous with unknowable. And although I understood it in only the dimmest way, my consecration to vision, to seeing, to spying out the land was sealed.

For can we, after all, average "the state in which we have been called"? Is there indeed an Everyman, dear to the heart of humanitarians, who contains the average of all our experience, the calculus of all our consciousness? Do we tote up the I.Q., the income level, the age, sex, siblings, color of eyes, and divide by a number of noses to arrive at the quintessence of a consciousness we call human?

I have no truck with gnostics, whether religious or scientific. Give me phenomena and plenty of it. Give me pictures and models of the cosmos, though I know them to be creatures of our consciousness. I'll take Heraclitus' everflowing stream, Democritus' falling atoms, Plato's harmonic spheres, Ptolemy's epicycles, Copernicus' sun caged by its circling planets. If the images of the atom as billiard balls or ricocheting waves prove inadequate, I am willing to wait for the new image of matter to emerge from its long-pent birth. The one thing I will not take is the denying darkness and the blind man's eye.

Where man is not, nature is barren.

—William Blake

I know I'm not seeing things as they are,
I'm seeing things as I am.

—Laurel Lee

Chapter IV

I know a man who had a tumor and, along with it, a sizable chunk of the right hemisphere of his cerebral cortex excised from his brain. He survived the surgery with no complications, woke up, functioned well, even talked to the doctors and nurses. There was only one problem: he was convinced he was dreaming. Nothing could persuade him that he was actually awake and aware. Descartes would have been proud of him. Perhaps he would have gone on in this dream world forever if it hadn't been for television. He finally decided that his own mind could not possibly produce the meager and unsatisfying scenarios he found on the screen. If he had been dreaming, he would have made a better job of it.

All sorts of centers for specialized functions have been located in the brain: areas controlling vision, speech, hearing, muscular reactions. But the search for the residence of will, decision, and belief has yielded nothing. There is no place where the brain can be jarred by charged electrodes into believing or deciding. Slices of cerebral cortex may be extracted by surgery; brains may be battered in automobile accidents so that thinking is greatly impaired. Still, consciousness goes on. Thinking—the taking in, sorting, and interpreting of stimuli—is indeed localized in that slick, meandering gray matter we call brain. But where do we decide what to think about? And behind that, who directs the brain in its harvesting of sensory impressions that provide the material for thinking?

Our minds do not work in the haphazard way of a scavenger on the sea bottom. Obviously, not all the storm of stimuli bombarding our nerve endings at every moment gets stored in the brain as food for thought. Consciousness has already made up a shopping list before the brain ever begins its daily marketing. From all the photons, sound waves, sensations of heat and pressure, it filters the information it has been instructed to attend to. Wilder Penfield, the pioneer of experimenting neurosurgeons, has pointed out that no one ever learned a skill or remembered an experience unless he had attended to it, focused his brain on it. A mere random sampling of stimuli leaves no mark on the mind. And my friend with the carved-up cortex could have gone on dreaming his life away if he had not come to believe in his own consciousness.

We say we must pay attention, and the verb in the idiom is well chosen, because the cost of consciousness is immense. Focusing requires a fine grinding of the lens. The distortions must be discovered and, with utmost care, ground out. We sand down our sensibilities by a constant friction against the world, flaying our eyeballs with sights that can sear like the sun, rounding the curvature of the cornea with the glaze of alkaline tears. Pain is the price of paying attention. Even the pleasures we perceive are fleeting, and cause us the greatest grief of all. We are constantly saying good-bye to good.

Honing is a hazardous process. Scraped to the bone, we set ourselves up like lightning rods to catch the finest disturbance in the atmosphere. No wonder the demission rate is so high. Who wants to risk incineration, a brain burnt to a frazzle like an overloaded filament? Rimbaud, the French poet, had by twenty-one charred his cortex by trying to raise to the level of consciousness every single stimuli his senses were capable of assimilating. Even so, he said it was worth it.

But it is only brain most of us want, not consciousness. And in itself, the organ seems marvelous enough. Its endless compartments hold codes for the way to get to work, the way home again, what we like to eat, the names and faces of friends. Even when consciousness is suspended, the brain continues to function, although it may miss a few red lights on the way to the office. An epileptic suffering a *petit mal* seizure will continue to breathe, walk, open the door, sit down, though no memory remains of those actions. And most of us live our lives in a constant state of *petit mal* seizures. The difference is that epileptics have their brains blown about by unsought electrical storms whereas we decide to detach consciousness through a failure of nerve.

Memory itself seems to be in an intermediary position between brain and consciousness. What consciousness decides to pay attention to is coded in chemical structures called engrams. But they are not stored in any particular cell or area of the brain; they are diffused throughout the brain. Dispersed, non-local, they wash the cortex like an inland sea. And like sea water, any single cup can hold the clue to the composition of the whole. Karl Pribram's work on the structure of the brain gives evidence that memory is generally recorded all over the brain. Structure, in fact, implies too rigid a picture, at least for memory, which seems a fluid sort of phenomenon. For any single memory merges with other memories from different times, forms associations with present sensory excitations, changes the perceptual patterns, flows in what we call a "stream" of consciousness.

Our skull is like a cup holding this heady decoction of mingled memories, saved from decaying into chaos by the preservative of reason and kept brimming by continually new distillations from the senses. Few, I think, choose to bear such a cup, to stand under such a load.

For the load is just this: the creation, the fabrication of phenomena. Without perception, not only is there no crash as the tree falls in the forest, but there is no tree, no forest, no sound of any kind. Not the clicking of chitin-shelled insects in the quivering summer heat, not the call of birds stitching through the branches, not the tensile creak of the tree's raised column of water and minerals sprouting like a fountain in the wind. Not even silence.

Not that I doubt the world or think I'm dreaming. This is no Descartes who confides only in consciousness, who would cut the carnal cords that bind him to the earth and float free of phenomena. However one digs at the roots of the world—with quantum bundles of energy, with molecular galactic systems, with undulating fields of electromagnetism—the world is still out there waiting—pure movement, pure being. But in here, and only in here, sucked up by the senses into the nervous system and delivered crackling and popping to consciousness, it takes shape as tree, leaf, resin, root.

WE tramped on the Blue Lake Trail in the Cache la Poudre Valley the day after Christmas, following the narrow bands of ice compressed by cross-country skis. The land, elaborate with underbrush and firs, rose and fell away, forcing us down diagonals and up along edges. Thirsty for the righteousness of rocks and what grows there, we could only sponge up so much stimuli before the overload built up, the cup we balanced brimmed and spilled. We unburdened ourselves by knocking the snow off a stump in a spray of infinite crystals and speaking. "Look," my companion says, "at all the trees God made."

And I reply in my own electrical storm, "You help him make them trees." You. And you are lifting the ink from this page, and alchemizing it into trees you've never even seen. You. The truest name for consciousness. Truer than Descartes' "I" because it reciprocates its own image, recognizes itself in reflection. This is how we most often address it. You. Yah. Hallelu-you.

One makes the woods he walks in. He takes the raw materials of reality spread before his senses, chomps out a bit here, a bite there, chews them up with the saliva of memory, swallows, and spits out "Tree!"—all in a split second, and while simultaneously taking a nip from what he will name "sky" and "snow."

Humankind is an organism for transmuting raw, undifferentiated energy into phenomena. Just as plants, on a theoretically less conscious level, transmute light into leaf. Plants make a properly slow, leisurely activity of it, although an elm at six million leaves per summer is no slouch. But a human, voracious and swift, images and caches a store of summers, inviolate in engrams in his brain. The various creatures of the universe move at different tempos but to the same music. In the harmonic spheres of the cosmos, we are at the nucleus of knowing, oscillating at incredible speeds.

We are the world's philosophers' stones, its means of making meaning. Without us, however hard the elm root sucks the soil, no single serrate leaf will be brought to light. Mere molecules may spin, faithful to their pattern, obedient to the order given them, unerring electricity. But no light-filtering mist of green appears, no wind of Newtonian mechanics lifts them lightly. They neither rustle in spring nor rattle in fall. They exist, but only in what we may best call undifferentiated being, I suppose, unless we prefer the words physicists make up and discard periodically to describe the farthest back thing that matter is. But being, pure and undifferentiated, or atomic particles or energy fields are colorless, tasteless, and mute. Unless or until they have an instrument to play upon. An Aeolian harp of human consciousness.

It is easy enough to imagine the world without us, scrubbed of cities, clean of our creations, clear of consciousness. In fact, it is often pleasant to do so. A pristine Eden, still uninfected by man. But it is impossible to imagine without a mind. We are able to shape a sphere, marbled and miracled, ourselves erased. But even that image lives only in our mind. Take away the mind and the bubble bursts, dissolves, drifts into inarticulate arrangements.

There are no phenomena without perception, no perception without attention, no attention without desire. Beauty is in the eye of the beholder, says the cynic. Precisely. But he says more than he knows. More elusive than engrams is a code in our consciousness that recognizes beauty when it sees it, that builds it out of molecular movement. But an even more elemental code desires, searches for, insists upon beauty.

Why do we seek out trails over rocks and through snowdrifts that do not accommodate for comfort? Why do we, at great difficulty and expense, search out experiences that provide totally intangible satisfaction? Because beauty is in our eye, itching like a curious conjunctivitis that refuses to be soothed until proper material is supplied it to sort, arrange, pattern, proportion.

Perception, especially visual perception, has been counted as one of the most passive occupations of human intelligence. Supposedly one simply opens his eyes and takes it all in. But the research of physiologists has shown the whole process to be one of continual interaction with the environment. The eyeball itself is undergoing small, steady, rapid vibrations, shifting the image received on the retina by the microscopic distance that lies between its adjacent cells. Added to that rapid oscillation is a slow drift of the image across the retina, continually corrected by a flick, like a typewriter carriage being flung back to its starting point. When these normal movements of vision are impeded in an experiment using a series of mirrors, sight first becomes distorted and finally fails altogether. The researchers discovered that the nerves must constantly participate in an interchange with light, must probe and feel the image presented to it. If the stimulus supplied to each retinal cell is kept constant, the nerves learn to accommodate the stimulus, and it soon falls below the level of perception. The eye, in other words, must toss light about as if it were winnowing wheat from chaff, sifting, sliding, flicking it, in order to garner shape, distinction, color, form.

Nor is perception merely a matter of present stimuli assaulting the senses. Put on a pair of distorting spectacles that make straight lines look curved and walk into a strange room. At first the result is utter sensory confusion. What you see isn't what you're getting. But before long you will be able to move about accurately, undeceived by the images actually being recorded on your retinas. Indeed, you will cease to "see" the curves at all; they will straighten themselves out in your mind, even though the data taken in by the optic nerve remain curved. The same thing happens with people given spectacles that invert images: they quickly learn to "see" right side up again.

Part of the ability to adjust for distortion is a product of memory. It is partially achieved by the interplay of kinesthetic and visual senses. The point here is that the optic nerve does not simply transmit a copy of the image to the retina. It selects, emphasizes, even discounts data. Sometimes it "sees" what is not even there on the retina at a particular moment.

We are not mere blank tablets being written upon, scored and splotched by stimuli. Perception is not a simple matter of taking sense impressions the way film emulsion takes pictures inside a camera. We do not see only what is right before our eyes; there are much more accurate analogies for describing perception. In one of them we are likened to directors constantly casting parts for the theater of our minds, what Bohm calls the "inner show" that the brain presents to consciousness as reality. The retina scouts about for likely actors. They are put on stage probationally, asked to turn this way and that to show what sort of stuff they're made of. And consciousness, sitting back in the darkened director's corner of the theater, decides. Some of the parts are found to be discordant and demand a reconciling adaptation. Others are discovered to be false entirely, unsuited to the overall drama.

Or perception is like a dance. We engage our surroundings in a spinning, drifting matrix of matter and mind. Shall we dance? The elm lifts its leafed arms and we fall into them, clicking our retinal heels, arabesquing among the branches.

Perception demands participation, not detachment. We've fooled ourselves for several centuries now, thinking our proper place was one step removed, on the sidelines, observing like a wallflower. We thought that clear-headed perception of phenomena required that we not be swept off our feet, that we stand aside, even outside. And art, too, invented a mechanism to match this detached ideal of science. We called it perspective because we believed we had finally *seen through* everything, seen through the world's ruse of meaning.

"There was a time," H. G. Wells once remarked, "when my little soul shone and was uplifted by the starry enigma of the sky. That has now disappeared. I go out and look at the stars in the same way I look at wallpaper." This is the extreme disengagement from physical reality that began simultaneously in the arts and in science. Looking at stars as wallpaper was incipient in Francis Bacon's pronouncement in *Novum Organum* that "nothing really exists except individual bodies, which produce real motion according to law; in science it is just that law, and the inquiry, discovery, and explanation of it, which are the fundamental requisite, both for the knowledge and for the control of Nature."

Perspective is the visual representation of that mental trick of disengagement from the world. It recreates a way of seeing that places the eyes of the individual viewer at the center of a spatial sphere. It is a device not, as we usually assume, for imitating or reproducing reality, but rather for underscoring depth and separation in space. During the Renaissance, the point from which the world was viewed wavered, swerved, and finally staggered outside the picture frame. Bacon's individual bodies viewed other isolated bodies with detachment. The space that lay between them became only a void; space was defined as merely the absence of phenomena. With perspective there was no participation, no engagement of the world, only the rigid rails of geometry disappearing at the horizon, carrying off the cosmos into oblivion.

Had no one ever noticed perspective before? Had centuries of artists been so blind, so witless as to ignore the way the world *really* looks? Or was perspective simply a visual convention that did not fit what they found to be significant about reality? To Bacon and his inheritors, separation was significant. For the millennia of artists, both pagan and Christian, that went before, participation in and identification with reality was significant. In the Middle Ages, says Owen Barfield, paintings were done "as if the observers were themselves *in* the picture. Compared with us, they felt themselves and the objects around them and the words that expressed those objects, immersed together in something like a clear lake of—what shall we say—of 'meaning,' if you choose."

Space as a mindless, lifeless void had no place in any of man's cosmologies before the scientific revolution. Before that, not only did the bushes burn, the serpent speak, and the trees clap their hands, but the ether, that vast, ineffable ocean in which we were all submerged, trembled with intelligence. Then came the drought, the four hundred years' temptation in the desert. We became accustomed to living in a wasteland where life receded steadily from being, and being receded from space. In our collective mind's eye, subject shrank from object. Our feet faltered, the music stopped, we fell out of the tree, the dance was over. The image of Bacon's individual bodies, reduced to external relationships, ruled our imagination. Empires broke into nation-states, matter into atoms, psyches into compartments of consciousness, the body into systems.

Nowadays we look back and see even the past in perspective. We feel acutely our separation from that primitive perception of the world. Unlike our animistic forebears, we are not at home in the world nor in the picture. And we diagnose the case to favor our own symptoms: they were the victims of a delusion that projected a consciousness upon a dumb, drooling cretin of a cosmos, and God was only a melancholy, wish-fulfilling reflection of themselves. But was God an anthropomorphic fantasy, or have we become mechanomorphic nightmares? Without our paying much attention to how we got here, we have come to the point of talking about our bodies as marvelous machines, our minds as computers, our behavior as mechanisms.

"Theory" and "theater," however, are sibling words stemming from the same parent. At root they both mean "seeing place." And theoretical scientists are those who stage possibilities for the "inner show," who crawl back through the proscenium arch to put their imaginations into the picture again.

Joshua Lederberg, a Nobel prize-winning biochemist, describes how he went about making his laboratory discoveries, which were as much a function of the imagination as of rationality:

> One needs the ability to strip to the essential attributes of some actor in a process, the ability to imagine oneself *inside* a biological situation; I literally had to be able to think, for example, "What would it be like if I were one of the chemical pieces in a bacterial chromosome?"—and to try to understand what my environment was, try to know *where* I was. . . .

Now that is hardly looking at stars as wallpaper. Such diving inside among the twining ropes of chromosomes through the agency of consciousness is an act of phenomenal participation in reality.

And lest we leave consciousness to the waking hours only, consider the testimony of Friedrich Kekulé. He discovered the molecular structure of organic compounds while dreaming. How did they appear to him in this dream? He saw the atoms "dancing."

It seems the question of whether one clump of matter can observe another clump of matter is moot after all. That's not an adequate description of what's going on here. We're not *observing*, Heisenberg, we're *dancing*. Locked in an embrace with the world, our retinal cells quivering at the approach of the pulsating photons like any giddy girl at the prom, we are ourselves phenomena dancing with phenomena. No more looking at things in perspective, artfully abstracting ourselves from the situation as though we feared rejection, feared finding no partner. We are a little clumsy, it's true, and have forgotten most of the steps. We're inhibited and more than a little embarrassed at throwing ourselves into the arms of the universe with such abandon. Other peoples seem to have mastered the necessary interpenetrations of the movements more successfully than we of the West, who are understandably rusty after so many centuries of trying to act like machines. Many of us rush off to find foreign dance masters at the expense of losing our own long-neglected lore.

Still, the great thing is to say yes to the invitation.

David Bohm defines science as "basically a mode of extending our *perception* of the world, and not mainly a mode of obtaining *knowledge* about it." What we have in the past taken for knowledge about the world is merely an abstracting of a single configuration in the pattern of the dance, and calling that the last word on reality. We're only just discovering the impoverishment of the kind of vision that mistakes stars for wallpaper. "For in science too the totality of the universe is too much to be grasped definitively in any form of knowledge," Bohm concludes, "not because it is so vast and immeasurable, but even more because in its many levels, domains, and aspects it contains an inexhaustible variety of structures which escapes any conceptual 'net' we may use in trying to express their order and pattern."

MY dog died the other morning on the floor beside the bed. As the last of his mortal breath rattled his throat and his eyes glazed over like tough gelatin, I knew that what he had been wasn't there any more. A corpse lay beside the bed, something that once had been a dog but now was only short-hand, an abbreviation, a sign with "dog" printed on it, growing stiff as a cipher. My dog was—is—more than I know, more than all the coded engrams for him my brain has collected over ten years' time. There were, for example, all those hours—days, even—when I was not particularly conscious of him, when I did not, could not pay attention. He caught my wandering awareness from time to time with a deep, disgusted sigh and a desultory flop of his tail. Did my attention call him into being, or at least into *more* being? Is that why he so often demanded it? Was he non-existent when I wasn't look-ing? These are precisely the questions physicists ask them-selves today about bits of matter smaller than a medium-sized mammalian. And the answer has something to do with C. S. Lewis' contention that our dogs will be "raised" in us as we are raised in Christ.

Certainly my dog had being as molecular movement, just as I do. But as another writer has pointed out,

> molecular movement is not sound; molecular movement is not light. The vibrational effects—or whatever we wish to call them—are interpreted by *us* as sound and light. Could we see the waves or vibrations, *per se*, we would not see redness or blueness, loudness or music. Yet when cells in our brains begin to be shaken up in certain ways light and sound enter our minds.

It is at this point that phenomena are conceived. Or, as Ruskin put it, "Let there be light, is as much, when you understand it, the ordering of intelligence as the ordering of vision."

So the answer is yes. As a phenomenal dog he did depend on my attention. Or on the attention of the cat that was always pestering his ears and tail. Or perhaps, in some dim way, he depended on himself. Dogs are surely not as self-conscious as we, but they know enough to stage a little drama of their own to distract us from time to time.

Still, it is ourselves—alert, aware, attentive—who are the universe knowing itself, perceiving the patterns, imagining ourselves bacterial chromosomes or organic compounds, building the steely structures of Bach, finding the suburbs rasping the shape of beauty in our eye. And we are the ones who perceive the evaporation of consciousness in death and yet decide, in some place undiscoverable by spatial coordinates, to believe beyond the brain in the implication of consciousness.

Saint Paul, in that uncanny way saints as well as scientists have of staging possibilities before us, promised an interpenetration of consciousness, a participation in divine life. We live in Christ; he lives in us. The consciousness that upholds us in being, that attends us into being, that conceptualizes all the "levels, domains, and aspects" of the universe simultaneously, will expand, open its arms, and ask us to dance.

*The contemplation of this world
beckoned like a liberation.*

—Einstein

Chapter V

DOWN the hill from where I grew up lies a pond I always visit when I go home. The pond belongs to Mr. Locke, who lives in town and only fishes there occasionally. The upper skin of this pond, a turbid, living soup, is the color of tarnished quicksilver.

Last night a big wind blew from the north, and today pine needles, twigs, even limbs float on the sleek surface. The sun lies slantwise across the sky and strikes the pond tilted. Wakes like liquid arrowheads move across the water. Invisible fish roil the sheen. Microcosmic hurricanes spin over this inland Atlantic. Near the opposite bank, something—a copperhead or a turtle head—sticks up above the surface. Whatever it is, it was not there before, and when I look again, it is gone. A liquid blip, and some sly creature submerges. Crows—two—fly above the pond in figures, keeping as parallel as skaters except when one dips to nip its partner. Someone on the other side of the world's windowpane is inscribing these hieroglyphics for me to read.

Then all at once the light changes. Its amazing gyroscopic tilt is lost; it falls and flattens. The point is suddenly gone, removed from everything. A moment ago the scene was turgid with emergent meaning; now the pond yawns and turns its back on me. The stuff that floats on the surface is only debris, trash. And junk is stuff that has become, maybe always was, irrelevant, that has no connection with anything else. What I had thought were angles and patterns undergirding the very substance of the universe are only insect-infested yellow pines reflected trivially in the water. Why, I wonder, did I trudge down here? If you've seen one East Texas pond, you've seen them all. Mud and murk. So what?

I stand on the pier and sigh, my stomach turning over like a fish going belly up along the bank. There's no use trying to hold it together, to force significance on a trivial little pond that is only run-off water and decaying vegetation.

I am still standing there, drugged with ennui, when everything slips again—the sun drops another degree of arc, the kaleidoscope turns and proposes a new pattern. The pond opens to me once more, discloses itself. After a quarter of an hour, a sliver of time-pie, the leaves and twigs are forming a distinct, undeniable design on the surface of the water like magnetized needles, drawn by electrical charges to a compelling center. The painter Willem de Kooning once called himself a "slipping glimpser." Today I know what he means. Am I looking at the pond, or is it looking at me? After that hiatus in which I thought the whole world had died, it once more beats like a heart before my eyes. Occasion has slit the sides of the world, and I, like a surgeon, stare inside, entranced. It expands, springs out, inhales; contracts, tightens, squeezes.

Is it only a matter of time, then? Or of timing, of rhythm? If the fish, turtles, snakes, pine needles, trees, and clouds are embedded in the heavy mercury of the lake, I am embedded —must live in—days and hours.

A hummingbird's wings flutter forward and back fifty to seventy-five times a second; bees' wings, one hundred ninety times a second. Human beings can't even see that fast. The smallest segment of time that we can take in and digest as time is one-tenth of a second. Nothing shorter than this can be experienced as what we call a "moment"; we cannot distinguish changes that take place in less time. This is our unaided perceptual limit, the shape of our peculiar pond. So bees' and birds' wings blur across our eyeballs; we cannot observe each individual beat.

The heart of a shrew, like that of many small, furry animals, beats up to 800 times a minute. Such creatures experience more in an hour than we do in a day. They would laugh at our idea of what constitutes flying time. For them the present is a smaller portion, a hundredth of a second; a day is like a year. Their whole lifetime passes in a matter of months. If time runs out so much faster for small mammals than for us, think of fruitflies measuring their generations in days. Or exotic elements produced in cyclotrons whose existence is measured in thousandths of a second.

Perhaps I have actually been standing on the pier of this pond for ages. Perhaps empires have risen and fallen while I waited for the light to come again. Stars die, and their corpses are found light years later striking some pond's surface. A cesium molecule oscillates 9,192,631,770 times, and we call that a second. Or at least we have since 1972. Before that a second was a segment of a minute, which was a segment of an hour, which was the unit with which we measured days. But our day is now an hour longer than a dinosaur's day was. And when the chambered nautilus first began building its stately mansion, the day was only made of twenty-one hours. Time is a slippery element.

In 1964, David Bohm was convinced that physics had but one absolute to deal with: the speed of light. Space and time had already fallen as the absolute structures that Newton had imagined. Both had been shown to be contingent on, limited by, each other. Paradoxically, the faster a bit of matter whizzes along, the slower time goes for it, until, as it approaches the speed of light, time stumbles and stands still altogether. The speed of light itself, however, was found to be equally measured by any observer stationed at any point. It was seemingly absolute. Light, it appeared, was the ultimate, irreducible measure for time.

The maximum speed for the propagation of a signal could be no faster than the speed of light. To imagine anything faster would be to turn time backwards—or inside out. One could never go so fast as to catch up with oneself again. Therefore time, though relative to other aspects of reality, could only go forward. One could not shuffle the past and the future about. One gets hungry, eats, and is satisfied, in that arbitrary order. To say otherwise is to throw out the concept of cause and effect. Bohm wrote:

> We see then that as long as we accept Einstein's theory of relativity it leads to an absurdity to suppose that there is any action through physical contact capable of constituting the basis of a signal that is transmitted faster than light. In other

words, either we have to assume that no physical action faster than light is possible, or else we have to give up Einstein's form of the principle of relativity. But thus far this form of the principle of relativity has been factually confirmed. Besides, as we have already seen, no physical actions have ever been discovered which are actually transmitted faster than light (e.g., material objects cannot be accelerated to the speed of light, because this would require infinite energy, while no fields are known which propagate influences faster than light).

In the same year, however, John Bell propounded his theorem that has even yet to be fully assimilated by physicists. There is indeed something faster than the speed of light, it seems. Subatomic particles do indeed operate in some other domain than the one we so smugly learned to call the space-time continuum just a few short decades ago. The other domain affects scientists much the way the looking-glass world affected Alice. It pulls the rug out from under everything we have understood as rationality. Cause and effect, with its billiard balls thwacking one another in predictable trajectories, now appears in the domain of particle physics a clumsy, provincial sort of notion. For in the subatomic world, the billiard balls all seem to know *simultaneously* their parts in the game, their steps in the dance. They don't sit around like bumps on a log, waiting to be knocked for a loop. Faster than the speed of light, intelligence is passed around, the particles gyre in concert like an incredibly accelerated school of fish or flock of sparrows. This is telepathy on what we have come to think of as an inorganic, dead, deaf-and-dumb level.

The universe is dancing. And the smallest bit of matter knows, unerringly and interiorly, the dance. Let there be no more talk of flashing signal lights. No more solitary figures sending out messages in quantum bottles to be picked up light years later on some distant star. No more cumbersome cosmic intelligence network dependent on the measurable flight of photons. The timing of this dance must take into account something more than the speed of light. It must take into account a "knowing" universe.

Bohm, surely a scientist possessed of Emerson's "transparent eyeball," was quick to envision new ways for the world to be, ways that Bell's Theorem opened up. "There is the germ of a new order here," he wrote in 1973. "This order is not to be understood solely in terms of a regular arrangement of *objects* (e.g., in rows) or as a regular arrangement of *events* (e.g., in a series). Rather, a *total* order is contained in some *implicit* sense, in each region of space and time."

The operation of that kind of total order is perhaps beyond discovery, although physicists are developing various metaphors for it. Certainly the metaphor of Jonathan Edwards, the colonial American theologian, is as good as any: "God's *preserving* created things in being is perfectly equivalent to a *continued creation*, or to his creating those things out of nothing *at each moment* of their existence." Bohm calls this capacity of the physical world not to stumble over its own feet, this faster-than-light elegance, an "implicit sense." As invisible as thought, but swifter. And perhaps it *is* thought, thought fleeter than the electrical impulses our own thoughts depend on. As Edwards described it, "That which truly is the substance of all bodies is the infinitely exact and precise and perfectly stable idea in God's mind, together with his stable will that the same shall gradually be communicated to us, and to other minds, according to certain fixed and exact established methods and laws." God thinking up the universe and distilling his thought, design, and information into each bit of the "substance of all bodies."

We have so identified time with clocks that we operate as though the machine manufactures the reality, ekes it out to us in divisible segments. The mechanism holds hostage our image-making about the world. One thing, we think, must bump into another in order to make it move. This applies to photons as well as to billiard balls, to Einstein as well as Newton. The lever catches and releases the cog, manufacturing time by the tick. And our delight at getting our hands on the controls of this mechanism we named the universe has blinded us to the frailty of the analogy. Even our own minds and bodies we most often describe nowadays in terms of mechanisms, ignoring their organic, pond-like nature.

But if we are to assimilate this new information about the world, the machine will have to be junked. There is something more here than it can measure. What that is all but baffles our imagination. "God knows," even physicists are tempted to say, throwing up their hands. Exactly.

Things, the objective, created stuff of the cosmos, have meaning in much the same way—only more so—that words do. Or, to make the verbal structure stronger, things mean as words mean. We speak words; God speaks things. He opens what we suppose to be his metaphorical mouth, and out tumble trees, viruses, moons. From his lips pour blood and water and wisps of clouds. Tse-tse flies and ptarmigans trip from his tongue. Whereas we can only say "is" or "equals," he utters the essential verb: be. Let there be. He means what he says and says what he means. "There are no misunderstandings in nature," said Jung, "anymore than the fact that the earth has only one moon is a misunderstanding." Creation means itself precisely and exactly. A rose is a rose is a rose. It does not dissolve into confusion around the edges. It is, of course, syntactically related to every other language particle in the great God-speech. To say that it means itself does not imply that one can cut it out, excise it from its context, and have it retain its meaning, any more than a heart can be cut out of a living body and continue to beat.

Scientists, writers—spies—have to stalk and ambush, wrestle and gouge out whatever meanings they can in this welter of the world. God can be obvious; they have to be cunning.

It is God who thinks the whole, rounded thought of the universe. And as one thought, its nature, its total order, is indeed implicit. Or perhaps he whistles it or sings it. Harmony only happens when the totality of the tune is known. The time signature varies with the demands of the creation. Adagio, presto, andante.

A hummingbird lives a different time than ours. Likewise a star or a mastodon.

It is time, ticking time, that defeats us. Not hummingbird time nor star time nor mastodon time, but the false picture we have of time manufactured, extruded, from a machine. We speak as though time were a commodity, or something, like money, to spend. The sun stood still for Gideon, yet today we rarely realize that not only do we live in time but time lives in us, a part of creation, the thinking-up of God. I have seen mornings stretch out before me like a huge expanse of level sea, endlessly unfolding, where I could have gone on forever. And I have had others close up about me so tightly I could scarcely turn around before they were exhausted.

Does time fly? And where to? All good things come to an end. A good end?

Ask the five wise virgins waiting for the bridegroom, their lamps brimming with oil. Or even the five foolish ones who had the door slammed in their faces. They knew to their sorrow that the feast was going on, unimpeded, just the other side of the door. Life was arranging itself in patterns there; the senses were going about the business of making sense. The bridegroom was magnetizing the revelers who swirled about him in the wedding dance. But on the outside was darkness, chaos, death of sense. The wailing and teeth-gnashing of madness.

"Watch, therefore." For life in time is not a stumbling from one ecstatic epiphany to another. The enormous task is to keep your eyes open, your wick trimmed, your lamp filled, your powder dry. Even when the bridegroom tarries. Even when the sky falls into the pond and the pond itself is sucked down some sewer of time that comes to nothing. Even when it all flattens out to triviality. Or the midnight cry, "Behold, the bridegroom cometh!" will catch you sleeping, your lamp overturned, the oil spilled out.

And then it is better if you had never been born. The moment you've been waiting for, the end for which you were made—your time—flies without you. Instead of going out to meet the bridgroom, glorious and infinitely desirable, you're in town haggling with the oil dealers. Life himself passes you by. The light dies out. The pond turns its back, closes the door. Depart. It doesn't know you anymore.

There are no two ways about it. You've got your eyes open or you don't. You're watching at midnight or you're not. You must be ready when it comes flying at you, skimming swiftly over the surface of time.

The cares of this world are no excuse. Not father, mother, wife, nor children. Not burials or births or weddings. Not fixing formula, scrubbing the toilet, peddling pills or prose. Whatever the great human enterprise currently in hand, the point is to watch. All the rest is addenda. Seeking the kingdom is the essential integer.

Keep your eyes open or you might as well be dead. You already are.

Some of us find it impossible just to stand around breathing and gawking. We must fidget with one thing or another that generally results in what we call society. The wise virgins among us strike the rest as odd. We call them contemplatives, hermits, nuts. We're a little put out with them because they refuse to take our fidgeting too seriously. And it doesn't seem fair that they should just sit and watch while the rest of us toil and spin our thin thread of virtue. No doubt the foolish virgins also thought their oil-hoarding sisters unfair. And the one who had to bury his father, please his wife, count his cows? Well, you can't keep your eye on everything at once.

Some few decide, out of a strange mixture of guile and zeal, to devote themselves to watching. They throw over their fathers, their would-be wives, their uncounted cattle. They fill their lamps and settle down to watch. They are undistractible. Their hungry eyes devour everything; they are starved for seeing.

If you plan to live this way, you better make up your mind early. Foolish virgins seldom stay virginal long. And undivided attention is impossible in the hubbub of the hive. He who takes a wife and child hath given hostages to fortune, said Thomas Hobbes, a not particularly devout philosopher. He recognized too late the advantages of the cloistered consciousness. Those who watch for the bridegroom are necessarily virginal and unswervingly single-minded.

But suppose you, young and foolish and palpitating in the lush spring air, have taken up having babies, stirring soup, humming to yourself, having mistaken one desire for another? Then life must go the long way round. Through the needle's eye.

There are the thousand daily deaths to die, the making of a frustrated living, cares to be taken. Adam's curse and Eve's. Sweat of the brow mixed with the daily bread; tears and blood that are the baby's bath. To a large extent the whole of Jewish culture is a gigantic effort to salvage something from this inheritance, to redeem these hostages we've given to fortune, to make the whole enterprise of earning a living and raising a family mean more than one long detour from Eden.

Only a nun can afford the luxury of loving mankind in general. The rest of us are stuck with particular specimens. A mendicant may wander the byways and backwaters without anxiety; no one is ever waiting for him at home, vexed or anxious over his lingering. Anne Morrow Lindbergh declares that there are so many women in church because it is the one hour of the week when no one can call "Mother!" The respite most women taste in the sanctuary for only an hour is the continual reward of the wise virgins on the far side of the door. That hour, out of the week's one hundred sixty-eight, is their needle's eye.

Thoreau, that Concord nun, threw away the pretty piece of limestone he had on his mantelpiece because it distracted him by requiring dusting. He had no doubt taken warning from his friend and mentor Emerson concerning the heart held hostage by family ties. When Emerson's firstborn son died at six, darkness such as the celibate can never know descended on him. It was a man pinned and wriggling in the needle's eye who wrote, not long after his son's death,

> There are moods in which we court suffering, in the hope that here at least we shall find reality, sharp peaks and edges of truth. But it turns out to be scene-painting and counterfeit. The only thing grief has taught me is to know how shallow it is. That, like all the rest, plays about the surface, and never introduces me into the reality, the contact with which we would even pay the costly price of sons and lovers.

Those of us who, one way or another, have ended up with a life that demands taking thought for the morrow must be grateful even for the escape offered in the needle's eye. And for its tag-end promise without which we might lose heart: with God, nothing is impossible. Not even the necessary shrinking to a single filament that will fit through that aperture. If the door is shut, then we must somehow struggle through the keyhole.

I open my eyes on the morning, and it is already in full flight. A crow, raucous across the pasture, is ridiculed by a wry mockingbird. A weaning calf bawls down the hill. Mist sifts up from the pond through the pine trees; above them, planes are ascending like lumbering luminous angels. People who are already at work in that early morning smugness feel the peculiar light that reflects from surfaces as yet unblunted by noise and bustle. The world is rushing away on the multiplied lines of a Minkowski diagram of time. Like any square meter of earth you dig up, it sustains life at all levels, a million myriad perspectives.

The answer to what's going on here is this: more than you'll ever know. But all I have to do to keep up with it is open my eyes. I stretch and inspect my soul, retinal cells oscillating, ganglions going full speed, structural perceptors probing, matching, discarding, repairing frayed hypotheses. This is the morning and this is me embedded in it, like a flounder lying flat and low in the mud of the bay, both good eyeballs wallering upward at what's going on, throat swallowing silt and spitting out the bones of being, upon which I shall presently hang some fleshed-out meaning.

This is my needle's eye: to lead this double life of working and watching, and yet to keep my eye single. No, I don't spend my days like Jerome or Thoreau, reeling through the underbrush, eyes starting from my head, tongue aflame. Yes, there are people waiting for me, people waiting to be buried, waiting to be pleased, wanting to borrow oil. I shall spend the time picking up things in one place and putting them down in another. Food, cups, money, paper, dust, words. But always in my mind's eye is the needle's eye, that tenth part of a second when I snare the implicit sense, the stable will buried in the world's body, when I turn and find myself staring at the Bridegroom.

*The life of spies is to know,
not to be known.*

—George Herbert

Chapter VI

Do I have a right to my double life? The question nags at me. It is one thing to openly declare yourself a mad scientist or a marginal contemplative so that the rest of society can take precautions against you. But it's quite another to go about disguised as an ordinary citizen, making your contributions of children, taxes, and casseroles while all the time you're up to something quite different.

There is Mary and there is Martha, but do they have a license to live within the same skin?

I have in mind an evening late in January. We, along with other guests, are watching the Super Bowl at the house of friends. The hostess is an alcoholic. One of the other guests is a retired Air Force recruiter whose nervous combativeness makes everyone a little uneasy. We sprawl on recliners and rugs, whooping or groaning at the game. At intervals we unwrap ourselves from our afghans and pad across the floor in our stocking feet to load our paper plates with fancy food. We are doing the same thing that millions of others are doing across the nation, participating in its consolidated life. At least that is our ostensible business.

But there is one among us, who puts a hand into the dish with the rest, who is a traitor to this open, honest fellowship. This person is not really watching the game or absorbed in the intermittent conversations about permanents or interest rates, although she appears to be. No. She is taken up with studying the incredibly bright turquoise of her hostess's eye, and with observing the delicate balance between permission and authority that the retired recruiter so unexpectedly maintains with his son. These are the situations into which I burrow like a mole.

When the talk at halftime turns to elections and gun control, I have no opinions to offer and pay little mind to those of others. But I love to watch them as they talk. The color rising and suffusing the faces, the eyes dropping, a palm opened and drawn back. The body telling the implacable truth. The recruiter's fierce, dark face compels my attention not because of his survivalist sentiments, but because it contrasts so peculiarly with the surprising gentleness he shows his son. He nestles the half-grown boy against his knees and strokes his fine, mouse-colored hair.

When the hostess confides in me about her family, the intensity of my gaze is grappled to those amazing blue-green irises set in her head like living stones. I know she is deceived and thinks me a better, more sympathetic person than I am. In fact, I am not really concerned over the woman's worries. But no matter. If the kingdom of heaven, toward which I am struggling through the needle's eye, is buried in that aqua iris, I will have it out.

It is the unspoken, unregarded elements of the evening—how the cold, blue darkness descends on us in the unexpected early evening, and how the room is shrunk by the sudden yellow lamplight—that I see, attend to, love.

This is the double life. This is my treason toward mankind: refusing to enter into the compact to pursue a happiness too small, too circumstantial.

Hiddenness has always been an attribute of the holy, at least in this world. "Truly thou art a God who hidest thyself," the desperate heathen around Isaiah complained. The kingdom is buried in the field, hidden in the measure of meal, sown while we sleep. God is a thief, slipping through the shadows. And I am a spy, hot on his trail. I cannot afford distractions. I cannot continually be making self-conscious explanations. "Please hold your tongue while I look at the light in your eyes, the lines around your mouth, this embodiment of beauty and sorrow." So I must pretend to listen. Deception is not a moral issue here, but the spy's device.

Still, I have my fears. And when I crawl into bed that night I am quaking and cold. What sort of monster am I, anyway, to make it my business to have no opinions, to want only to *see*? What right have I, after all, to go about digging up the field in my obsessed search for the treasure, leaving the land behind me looking like a minefield? Gouging out the eyes of witless women, invisibly inserting myself between father and son to intercept whatever truth lurks there? The bearer of those incredible turquoise eyes is bent on destroying herself. The recruiter is a man at war with himself. Are they nothing more than interesting to me? A momentary sop for my swollen curiosity?

I have, I realize, withdrawn my allegiance to the human enterprise. That's why I call myself a spy—because I am a traitor to my society. There's no point in disguising that fact. I have cut myself off from its comfort and rewards. And if one day, like John the Baptist, I find my head upon a platter for my pains, eyes still staring, I will not blame Herod or the headsman, who after all will only have rewarded treason as it deserves.

The work of Herod, it seems, is to teach people not to ask too much. Money is not too much to ask, nor is comfort, power to make decisions, aesthetic pleasure, family security—causes that will enhance life for a large or small group. You put your eggs in that basket. And for better or worse, according to the strength of your society, you reap the rewards of that choice. Because you have not asked too much. It is within the power of the human enterprise to grant the rewards, to some if not all. And if Salome gets half of Herod's kingdom, that is her due recompense for saving us from the desert madman who implored us to hunger for the whole kingdom.

My fear of asking too little is greater, I find, than my fear of my own immorality. I don't want something to make into a tidy little life for me and mine; I want Life itself.

One must be willing to risk immorality as a spy, to sin, as Luther advised, boldly. With a spy there can be no divided loyalties; the single eye is everything. The very goodness of good activities can be seductive. One must, in the end, be content to let the dead bury the dead, to stop one's ears to the voice of the mother and brothers and sisters that stand outside and call, "Come out, come back. Give up this strange obsession with staring and stalking, this mean hoarding of your oil. Share with us." But there are no half measures. One must either sacrifice or hoard.

Yes, I have a family, a house, a cat. I sit close to my fire on January evenings as you do. But I know these cozy comforts, taken in themselves, are finally futile. They drain away into the darkness in only a few years. One irrational duplication in a gene's design as a cell divides, and it is a cancerous corpse that rocks before the fire.

Still, the fire, the house, the cat—these provide as good a place to spy as any. Domesticity makes a fine disguise. The housewife hiding the leaven in the loaf and finding the coin knows this.

Kafka vouches for the success of the stay-at-home spy:

> You do not need to leave your room. Remain sitting at your table and listen. Do not even listen, simply wait. Do not even wait, be quite still and solitary. The world will offer itself quite freely to you to be unmasked, it has no choice, it will roll in ecstasy at your feet.

That is the spy speaking, the one who knows how to sit and wait in unlikely places, ready to pounce on reality, should it choose to reveal itself.

And it does so choose. Those who seek do find, as long as the seeking is their first and consuming passion. The door does open, gives way even as the knuckles strike it. "We may ignore, but we can nowhere evade, the presence of God," C. S. Lewis wrote. "The world is crowded with Him. He walks everywhere incognito. And the incognito is not always hard to penetrate. The real labour is to attend. In fact, to come awake. Still more, to remain awake."

So do not drowse by the fire or nod off at the table, over-stuffed with Herod's feast. For what is Herod's feast compared to the Messiah's banquet? In fact, Solzhenitsyn, that seasoned enemy of Herod, exhorts us from his own experience to "own only what you can carry with you; know languages, know countries, know people. Look around you—there are people around you. Maybe you will remember one of them all your life and later eat your heart out because you didn't make use of the opportunity to ask him questions." How light the engrams of memory are, floating through cranial fluid. One can indeed carry the world itself with him in those coded chemicals. They make a lighter burden than Herod's feast grumbling through the gut. True, the spy must be ready to leave the cat sitting by the fire, to slip out of the house and into the cold night at a moment's notice. But always he carries the cat and the fire and the house with him because he has looked around, stayed awake, remembered. Because he has asked questions, he will be answered.

Another addition to the spy manual I am compiling, this time from Chesterton: "It is good that the average man should fall into the habit of looking imaginatively at ten men in the street even if it is only on the chance that the eleventh might be a notorious thief." In fact, the most notorious of thieves.

I admit that moral folk have taken me to task for my habit of looking imaginatively at my fellow citizens, of raising to mere literary whimsy what is only a constitutionally morbid curiosity. I should cultivate, I have been told, more respect for persons and less lust for the bare phenomena. And respect for persons is indeed one of those entirely admirable sentiments with which one cannot possibly quarrel. It is undeniably a quality one must develop if one is to be a moral creature.

But persons in the abstract are quite slippery and elusive. To work it out dramatically, I must capture some token, some fetish of their very flesh. Collect pared nails and hair clippings, if only in engrams. And you may be sure I treasure them as I do my soul.

Nathan Hale, perhaps our most revered national spy, justified his dubious occupation in a letter: "Every kind of service necessary to the public good becomes honorable by being necessary." I have to leave my vindication at that. Seeing, taking a good look, is at least as necessary to the public's health as collecting taxes or garbage.

I met an Ojibwa Indian at a monastery that floated on the undulating plains of North Dakota like a tall, lumbering ship. He was telling us about how he had tried to escape the task his father had left him of being a healer and a reliquary for the story of his nation, a story that is not quite the same as the Sioux's or the Chippewa's. He's not one for writing, and not many of his people are interested in listening to the story, but he carves figures out of native wood that are the characters in the story that no one wants to hear. This is his book, he says. Our category for him is sculptor—in fact it is in that capacity that he is visiting at the monastery—but he calls himself a spiritual leader.

He is not an old man, nor young either. He still has some of his eight children at home. I look at him while I listen, at his flannel shirt-front speckled, like a trout, with tobacco burns, at his work boots giving way to his feet, at his cavernous mouth and its single upper tooth banded with gold. He paces back and forth, trying to tell about his people, his life compressed into another layer of lignite beneath the Great Plains soil, like a dinosaur arisen from its coal bed to explain itself.

I look, too, at the good Scandinavians and Germans watching him. They lounge about the folding chairs, at ease here. They all have their own souls to cure at home out there on the prairie. At Minot, Center, Williston, and Jamestown they will be waiting on Sunday to hear the story of how the world holds together, of what's going on here.

In one of those sudden image reversals that usually afflict only the young schoolchild, I am not seeing the Ojibwa now, but his counterpart from the future, a nice Norwegian pastor in snagged and shabby polyester, specially imported from the Lutheran reservation, telling how he struggles to keep a story alive. There are not many left who listen, he says, even on the reservation. The audience is polite in the face of this artifact, maybe embarrassed at his claims to healing, but interested in his ceremony of words as collectors of antiquarian cosmologies.

I am not a prophet, only a victim of occasional dyslexia. I

know there are ghostly structures of power that compel the consciousness of multitudes, that hold the imagination captive. We fall into the habit of thinking that the world goes on because of Herod. Because citizens watch the news and vote for proper candidates and organize societies for saving things. But this, if one examines the evidence, is not the case at all. The world goes on because we continue to believe in it, to take a good look around and agree with God that it is very good.

Still, all our songs are those of sojourners; it was by the bitter waters of Babylon that the Israelites believed in Jerusalem. All our pictures are of what we have lost, which is why we are willing to listen to Ojibwa medicine men. We don't need maps for where we live. We know the way to the shopping center, the bank, the school. We need maps for what we hope for. It's *buried* treasure that needs a map, not the marketplace.

And perhaps it is best that the treasure is buried in the field or in the measure of meal. Those ghostly centers of power polarize our attention, it's true, and distract us. But the kingdom of God itself was once buried in a tomb for three days and did its most potent work undetected.

Do you think that a middle-aged Ojibwa medicine man is impotent in the modern world? That his mother earth and morning star have diminished to a museum oddity? That Dante's paradise has fallen from the sky and Babylon erased Jerusalem? The spy still believes in the potency of buried treasure, whether coal or Christ. Though it be lost to us, it is not lost to itself.

And the spy, whose exile is necessary to his commission, slinks outside the gate, map in hand, disguised not by his own subterfuge, but by the blindness of the very ghostly structures that overlook him. He is overlooking nothing, however; he is scouting the people in the street in hopes of glimpsing the notorious thief that always takes us unawares.

So should I look at you if we should meet, my eyes first encountering yours directly in one quick penetration, then dropping or sliding sideways until, slowly, lifting, without your noticing, my glance would play about your throat, nose, eyes, temples. I would keep very still but not stare. I would smile slightly as if to encourage your ease. And there would be your ear, exposed, glossy and curling inward like a shell's whorl. I would follow fondly each logarithmed curve. See where the hair sprouts on your neck. Judge, as if by testing with its weight upon my finger, its texture and lightness. And thrown back from every plane, from your brow, the attenuated tips of your lashes, the curl of your nether lip, the light would speed and penetrate my own eyes, implanting there a latticed engram: you. And I would remember.

*Scientists are building explanatory structures,
telling stories which are scrupulously tested
to see if they are stories about real life.*
—Sir Peter Medawar

Chapter VII

LET me review the case so far. The evidence, I admit, comes to me indiscriminately. That is the nature of clandestine investigations. One takes the word of Lucretius and Dionysius the Areopagite as willingly as that of Bohr and Heisenberg. A conversation overheard on a street corner can be as instructive as documents of the Royal Academy. Given a context, nothing is irrelevant. That must be a spy's conviction.

The case, then, stands thus: the question of what the world is made of, at bottom, eludes us. It is as though we have been deflected from that inquiry and are being spun toward another question—*how* is it made?

Just why has the enterprise of describing the matter that makes up the world broken down? Everything seemed completely under control as late as the end of the nineteenth century. The inheritors of Copernicus, Kepler, Galileo, and Newton were certain that the universe and the laws that governed it had been adequately described. Discrete bits of matter, minute versions of planetary systems, hummed away in stable and predictable orbits. Molecules made firm alliances of atoms—atoms which could be named and ranked according to the quantity of their electrons. It appeared that the only task remaining to physicists was to take the measure of matter with instruments of increasingly refined precision. The matter, literally and figuratively, was locked up. In 1900 Lord Kelvin proclaimed that there were only one or two remaining clouds on the horizon to be cleared away before the pure light of reason would completely reveal the world for what it essentially was.

As a culture, we are still living off the psychological capital squirreled away by that age of optimism in science. For almost a century now we have fed on the popular notion that the world is an open book wherein we can look up the cause or effect of any action and thus predict, plan, or control the universe. For the first time since Eden we have believed ourselves to be the lords of creation. Whatever we require or desire, we need only to rearrange the bits of matter into new configurations to make. We kill and we make alive. The dilemma about which to choose—life or death—is a moral question, undoubtedly difficult to resolve, but it has nothing to do essentially with our ability to comprehend the cosmos. Understanding the world and understanding ourselves are two different enterprises entirely. At times we may have despaired of our ability to understand ourselves, but we have not doubted our ability to analyze and explain our external environment.

In fact, there is still only a handful of the technological populations of the earth who even at this point realize the depth of this delusion. Much of the university research in physics today is bent on a certain practical mopping-up operation in quantum mechanics. It studiously ignores the theoretical uncertainties into which bolder colleagues are venturing. And certainly the ordinary citizen of technopolis has no idea that the perceptual rug is about to be jerked from beneath his feet—no more than the citizen of Copernicus' Europe or of first-century Rome had any idea their world was about to be turned upside-down. Niels Bohr once complained that an address he had given to a group of philosophers, composed largely of positivists, had sparked no embarrassing questions. The fact that no one in his audience was perturbed or disgruntled made him think he had not adequately presented his material. "Those who are not shocked when they first come across quantum theory," he said, "cannot have understood it."

It is not just a matter of having discovered smaller and smaller bits of matter as the instruments for measurement have been refined to greater and greater precision. If Einstein's theories of relativity along with quantum mechanics could indeed tie up all knowledge of the physical universe into a tidy little package so that we could say we understand the world, then all the experimental information we have shattered atoms to achieve would make sturdy, predict-able sense. But in fact it does not. A good part of our infor-mation about elementary particles cannot be organized under any previous set of laws about matter and the way it works. Moreover—and whether this is the cause or the consequence of our ignorance is itself uncertain—we do not yet even have an accurate or potent enough language in which to express the information yielded by experiments on elementary par-ticles.

One of the clouds on the horizon so blithely dismissed by the Lord Kelvin in 1900 had to do with the properties of light. A few years later Einstein conceived his special theory of relativity to explain in a revolutionary fashion how light, the rarest thing we know, worked. In his search he dis-covered that time was much more plastic than we had as-sumed within the rigid realm of classical physics. Time dilated and contracted. Relativity added another dimension, literally, to our understanding of the physical world: space-time.

Relativity was based, strangely enough, on an absolute: the speed of light. Whether one is standing still or moving toward or away from the source of light, its speed is always measured at exactly the same rate—186,300 miles per second. This, of course, differentiates it from any other "thing" in the universe. We will measure the speed of an oncoming car dif-ferently if we are standing still than if we are moving toward it. All other speeds are therefore relative to our own situa-tion. Except for the speed of light.

Moreover, nothing *can* go as fast as light, because to do so would be to leave behind the electromagnetic fields that hold the atoms together, just as sound waves are left behind by supersonic jets. The atoms of the accelerated object would then fall apart. Attaining the speed of light is not possible, then, for an object. As we move toward a ray of light, we can never get any closer to its speed. It continually recedes before us like the horizon. Its speed will always be constant, therefore, relative to us.

Time, however, becomes as fluid and changeable as light is firm and unvarying. The old notion of absolute time dissolves in this new order. Time intervals measure differently depending on how fast the chronometer itself is moving. There is no such thing as absolute time, unrelated to any specified point of reference. Only within a carefully defined frame can one measure time. Both the observer and the object must be traveling at the same rate of speed for time to remain constant. If one or the other changes its frame of reference, however, the time that can be measured also changes. Outside the frame, all temporal meaning falls away and disintegrates.

The same principle applies to measurements of length. A clock, a train, a rocket—all become foreshortened on the end facing the direction in which the object is moving. Compressed, as it were. The length of any rigid body, then, can be measured only in relation to its frame of reference. We now call "proper time" that time measured by a clock at rest with respect to the observer (which actually means moving at the same speed and in the same direction as the observer), just as we call "proper length" that measurement made under the same conditions. But we can say nothing at all about absolute time or length. In other words, there are as many "points of view" about what's going on in the world as there are intelligences to perceive it. The measurements we make can have no meaning to us apart from where we are standing, our own position and velocity in relation to what we are measuring. To get an absolute measurement of anything we would have to crawl outside the world altogether.

Thus the observer himself is of necessity a part of the system he is measuring. We cannot tell the dancer from the dance.

There is, of course, another problem here. Just what constitutes an acceptable "frame of reference"? How do we know where to draw the line? Where does the system we are observing begin and end? If its borders are only arbitrary, how valid are the observations made within them? Might there not be something further out, something outside the frame that is influencing what is going on inside it?

Of course. One cannot snip out little sections of reality for study like pictures from a magazine. In order to fully understand what is inside the frame, one must take into account ever-widening rings of context.

Einstein realized this early in his work and spent the rest of his life working on the problem. He called his answer the "unified field theory." He took the entire universe as the total field needed as a context for the explanation of any part of it. The field was necessarily continuous and indivisible. Therefore one could not, except as a kind of handy abstraction, speak of "particles." To do so implied separating the world into isolated bits of matter that could "interact," a description that was no longer valid or relevant.

Realizing that, Einstein attempted to construct a new model for understanding the universe with his unified field theory. Instead of speaking of particles of matter, he envisioned one huge electromagnetic field with regions of varying intensity. The regions of very intense field (what in classical physics would have been called objects), surrounded and cut off from other objects by space, he called "singularities." What made this theory different was his premise: the singularity is never cloven from its surroundings. The field shades from greater to lesser intensity, but the membrane of existence is never broken. The universe is one flesh, existing as an undivided whole.

What we call primitive cultures have always operated inside a similar construction of reality. And what we call sophisticated cultures—those observing physical phenomena from supposedly isolated intelligences—have named this conviction of unity "totemic principle" or "animism." According to anthropologists, primitive cultures do not see themselves as separate from the world they inhabit, or as intelligences abstracted from the external world. "Mana," or "being," is simply more concentrated in some regions than in others, much like the "singularities" in Einstein's electromagnetic fields. Individual persons or objects are, to the primitive mind, "stopping-places of mana." The anthropologist Levy-Bruhl explains,

> It is not correct to maintain, as is frequently done, that
> primitives associate occult powers, magic properties, a kind of

soul or vital principle with all the objects which affect their sense or strike the imagination, and that their perceptions are surcharged with animistic beliefs. It is not a question of *association*. The mystic properties with which things are imbued form an integral part of the idea to the primitive, who views it as a synthetic whole.

In other words, primitive cultures achieve effortlessly the conceptual reality of the oneness of the observer with the object that Einstein and others have validated as the scientifically verifiable case. Whereas Western societies have gone through an intermediary stage of dislocating consciousness from its surroundings, of breaking the world into discrete objects and quarantining their own consciousness from it, primitive cultures still retain their perception of the essential unity of all being, although they are without Einstein's means of expressing it. They apprehend directly the undivided wholeness of the universe that we must mentally struggle to understand, so dependent is our thinking on a model for matter composed of separated, solid bits.

But how can any finite physicist, proscribed as he is by the limits of his own time and space, ever hope to take the entire universe into his calculations? Despite the studied efforts of those of a pragmatic bent who dismiss such questions as "merely" metaphysical, this impasse with the universe still remains.

Philip Morrison, a theoretical physicist at MIT, has illustrated one of the limits of our finitude. He explains why time (that is, a sequential process such as mixing molecules of ink in milk) can never be reversed *in actuality*, even if it is theoretically possible in analytical calculation:

> My main point is to add that every classical statement of the laws of motion on any system necessarily leaves out a small physical perturbation, some δH, which cannot in principle be included for finite systems, and which in fact is always amply large enough to prevent a complete retracing. . . . Whenever we choose to place the system boundaries, *something* remains outside which, in sufficient time and for suitably complex systems, will wreck the extraordinarily delicate correlations of

positions with velocity upon which reversibility, for example, depends. . . . Note that only one system, the whole universe, could possibly exist without any external unknown perturbations.

Einstein worked for three decades on his unified field theory, trying to connect gravitational and electrical fields in coherent equations. He is generally considered to have failed in this effort. But he left behind this conceptual possibility— the picture of the universe as a pulsating single organism.

Einstein's wrenching of our minds into a new mode through his special theory of relativity was quickly followed by another perceptual revolution: quantum theory. Observers noted that light, and indeed any high-energy ray, was not absorbed by or released from metals in a continuous stream of waves, as had been previously assumed. Instead, it made these transitions from one state to another in discrete, indivisible packages of energy called quanta. A quantum or packet of electromagnetic energy, for example, is called a photon. It always comes in exactly the same size; one is indistinguishable from another. But a glob of energy that can be localized in space is getting very close once more to a particulate picture of the world, to thinking of matter as granular and discontinuous. How could this possibly be reconciled with the new description of atomic structures in terms of waves?

Some attempt was made to resolve the wave/particle conceptual schizophrenia by calling a quantum of energy a "wave packet." A wave packet is a short train of a few wavelengths that can be equated with a particle.

Here we have an intriguing double paradox. Matter presents to us this dual face, like a coin. On one side it seems to be particulate and boundaried. On the other it is wave-like and extensive through all of space. A seeming contradiction. But while our conceptualizing is coming apart at the seams here, it has been unified elsewhere. Whereas matter and energy were once thought to be two separate categories, two different "things," they have now been shown to be merely different aspects of the same "thing." Matter is compressed and relatively stable energy, and energy is a dispersed, excited state of matter.

The revelation of such a paradox at the bottom of the world relieved no one's discontent, however, except that of Niels Bohr. He simply named the nature of the paradox "complementarity," that is, two faces of physical reality that are at once mutually exclusive and necessary to one another. The undeniable fact was that under different experimental conditions, matter behaves sometimes like a particle and sometimes like a wave, depending upon how the experiment is set up and what one is looking for. Light "waves," for example, can be shown to interfere with or cancel out one another, just as ocean waves coming from different directions can meet and cancel one another. In addition, light defracts around the edges of impediments just as waves do. But to observe this wave-like character of light, one must set up the kind of conditions—for example, a double-slit experiment—that allows it to display this side of itself.

But another sort of experiment—say, the bombarding of certain metals by photons—shows that these bundles of energy are always absorbed and emitted in discrete quanta, not in one long, continuous wave-like stream. Therefore, both the photon (the quantum of electromagnetic energy) and the electron (the quantum of electric charge) are necessarily conceptualized as "elementary particles" even though both have also been observed in other experiments to behave as waves.

Another problem arises here with the appropriation of quantum theory. One of our most basic understandings of the universe involves the notion of cause and effect. It is the underpinning of all classical physics. One hits a ball, and it moves at a certain speed and in a specified direction determined by the direction and degree of energy one puts into the blow. Nothing could be simpler. (But it is simple only because we have had centuries of adapting to the notion of seeing the world in this way. It would not have been so obvious, for instance, to Aristotle.)

Now, however, we suddenly must contend with a whole

new picture of the world and thus a whole new interpretation of reality. It is this: a quantum of energy, whether electromagnetic or electrical charge, cannot be tracked continuously. An electron, for example, can be measured in the act of leaving the tip of the cathode. It can then be measured again as it strikes a target particle or film emulsion. But it cannot be traced "in flight," as it were. We can only assume that the electron moves continuously through the intervening space. We even have to assume that it is the same electron that leaves the cathode that strikes the target. What makes this so problematical is that there seems to be no way of predicting just where the electron will land. None of the classical equations by which one could predict the trajectory of a ball or a bullet work on this level. The electron cannot even be shown to "exist" between one point and the other. This is the often-used, if seldom understood, meaning of the term "quantum leap"—a jump between stationary states, a flicker here and a flicker there, rather than a continuous movement of a particle across space.

On the other hand, to try to trace the *wave* aspect of the electron as one would a moving particle is also impossible. To introduce any kind of measuring device into the situation would deflect the direction and/or distort the amplitude of the wave, just as a sea wall or a barrier reef will break up the continuity of incoming waves. We can only see to measure an object because the light bounces off the object and into our eyes or records on our measuring device. When we are measuring a large object such as a train or a pinball, the combined energy of all the light bouncing off its surface and into our eyes is not great enough to make any appreciable difference in the measurement. But when what we are measuring is light itself, the situation is somewhat different.

In a laboratory situation, a scientist may "see" or at least make a picture of the microscopic object he wants to observe by directing a beam of extremely small particles at the target. When they strike the object, these particles scatter and make a pattern related to the target, so that something can be known or at least inferred about the object. But when what one is observing is itself a photon or an electron, one cannot aim a beam of other photons or electrons at it and expect anything meaningful to emerge. For the shorter the wavelength, the higher the energy packed into it. And with each collision of the target particle with particles of comparable size, the course it *might* have traveled had it remained unimpeded by other particles becomes more distorted and less discernable. Once again, therefore, the detecting device cannot be divorced from the reality it tries to perceive.

"The 'quantum' context thus calls for a new kind of description that does not imply the separability of the 'observed object' and the 'observing instrument,' " insists David Bohm. "Instead, the form of the experimental conditions and the meaning of the experimental results have now to be one whole, in which analysis into autonomously existent elements is not relevant." He uses the metaphor of observing the pattern in a carpet. Insofar as what one is interested in *is* the pattern, to separate the various parts of the pattern—here a flower, there a tree—is not meaningful activity and will prove fruitless. To see the *pattern*, one must take it all in simultaneously. "Similarly, in the quantum context, one can regard terms like 'observed objects,' 'observing instrument,' 'link electron,' 'experimental results,' etc., as aspects of a single, overall 'pattern' that are in effect abstracted or 'pointed out' by our mode of description."

Though quantum theory and the theory of relativity are significantly different, they both share this implication of undivided wholeness, of the impossibility of isolating the observer from the world.

There remains one further worrisome implication inherent in quantum theory, one to which Einstein himself was never fully resigned. It involves substituting statistical descriptions of the natural world for descriptions of actual, individual events. The wave function of the electron can at best be located by a measurement of probability, since it cannot be measured in actuality. There is no possibility of predicting what will happen in detail in each experiment because the measurement of waves is always indeterminate due to their very nature. Quantum mechanics can only deal, then, in the statistical averages garnered from multiple experiments.

Given this limitation, the physicists de Broglie and Schrödinger developed equations that describe wave fields statistically. They identified the area around the nucleus of an atom where one would be *most likely* to find an electron. This kind of mathematical map proved quite valuable, and most physicists were satisfied to deal with their material on this level. With the aid of the equations, they had a high enough incidence of success to willingly leave the matter at that. But the price of accepting quantum mechanics as an explanation of matter and motion was the abandonment of the idea of cause and effect. One could not have it both ways. Still, most physicists were willing to pay the price and to settle for a merely statistical reality.

Werner Heisenberg, however, went even farther. He understood the statistical reality that quantum mechanics described as absolute. It was not just a matter of averaging the outcome of large aggregates of sub-quantum events. That, certainly, is how a philistine physicist might understand the situation. But Heisenberg, who had been a thoroughgoing Platonist from his youth, refused to ignore the philosophical implications of quantum theory. And he chose to explain them on a much deeper level than mere pragmatism provides.

Heisenberg made a fundamental division of the world into the "real" and the "actual." The atomic level of the world is indeed *actual* because it can and does act. But it is not *real*, as it is not made up of *res*, or things. To him, atoms and all their components are the sheerest mathematical Platonic forms. "Our elementary particles," he said, "are the original models, the ideas of matter. Nucleic acid is the idea of the living being. . . . They are representative of the central order." In other words, the structures of the atomic world are simply the purest thoughts we can think. And it is necessary to think these thoughts in an equally pure mathematical language. Words, pictures, and models taken from the realm of our gross sensory experience can only muddy and contaminate this realm of pure forms. On the most fundamental level, the world, according to Heisenberg, is an idea. Physics must concern itself, then, with the mathematical relationships, and not go messing about with models. " 'In the beginning was symmetry' is certainly a better expression," he says, "than 'in the beginning was the particle.' Elementary particles embody symmetries; they are their simplest representations, and yet they are merely their consequences."

Einstein, however, operated from a different philosophical base, perhaps even a different aesthetic base. Although realizing the value of his colleagues' work, he was not content with statistical description, and never admitted it as the ultimate and inevitable end of our knowledge. To him, quantum mechanics was not a closed system: "Some physicists, among them myself, cannot believe that we must abandon, actually and forever, the idea of direct representation of physical reality in space and time; or that we must accept the view that events in nature are analogous to a game of chance."

Theory with no link to physical experience had also been the Cartesian position. Perhaps Heisenberg's Platonic physics had a loftier aim than Descartes' physics. Long before Einstein, Plato aspired to climb outside the "cave" of the cosmos for a god's-eye view. Descartes sought to achieve the same effect merely by climbing inside his own skull. But cleaving thought from matter, excising form from content, the dancer from the dance, leaves us with a corpse dangling in our arms.

And in the end a Platonic corpse smells no better than a Cartesian one. In either case, the world is killed because it is despised. The shadowy images that make up this world were not good enough for either Plato or Descartes.

Einstein may not have been an observant Jew (although he certainly irritated several of his scientific colleagues by his constant commending of the cosmos to its Creator), but he kept a heroically Hebraic grip on matter. He steadfastly refused to give it up for any fancy Greek notions about pure forms. He insisted that the *embodiment* of Heisenberg's "ideas of matter" is what is essential to physics, and indeed to human understanding. And he stood a solitary guard over the world's body until he died.

I seem to have been only like a boy playing on the seashore, and diverting myself in now and then finding a smoother pebble or a prettier shell than ordinary, whilst the great ocean of truth lay all undiscovered before me.

—Isaac Newton

Any moral crisis is a crisis of colour, texture, blood and the elements, of speech, vibration, etc.—the materials with which art, like life, is constructed.

—Marc Chagall

Chapter VIII

Although Einstein became something of a folk hero in America before his death, among physicists his dissatisfied fiddling with quantum theory was dismissed as the fretfulness of an old curmudgeon. The question of the missing physical link between quantum mechanics and actual experience faded from their minds. Few physicists, however, were prepared to undertake the enterprise of describing the world on such a rarefied level as Heisenberg chose. But neither were they prepared to give up the amazing new toy of quantum theory. While they would not, or could not, accept probability on an absolute, Platonic level in the manner of Heisenberg, they were more than willing to accept statistical descriptions as a compromise between uncontrollably variant numbers.

Heisenberg's wife Elisabeth had expressed a fear that the generation of physicists following her husband and his colleagues would ignore the wider context of quantum theory, and would indeed interest themselves only in details, much as the astronomers of late antiquity were content to predict eclipses using cycles and epicycles, eventually forgetting all about Aristarchus' heliocentric theory. Heisenberg himself had already noted a decided shift toward pragmatism in physics, particularly in America, where most of the postwar research was likely to be carried on.

One of the central questions for those interested in the wider context, however, became this: Do we settle for statistical descriptions because it is presently impossible for us to accurately measure each component in an experiment, or do we accept them because there is a certain amount of irreducible lawlessness at the bottom of the universe that by its nature is unpredictable? Is there a certain amount of "accident" or static that is regrettable but unavoidable? Is the whole construction we call the universe actually sitting on a bed of rubble?

Are there hidden variables, elusive of our discovery but still governed by laws, that make electrons not quite predictable? Or is there a certain residue of chaos clinging to creation that accounts for its uncertain behavior if one peers at it too closely? Would we, if we are wise, continue simply to add and divide events in order to describe phenomena, whether electrons or suicide rates? If we search too hard for the individual electron or stare too long at the face of the solitary suicide, will we find our question is unanswerable—in fact, without meaning?

This is exactly the conclusion a goodly number of pragmatic physicists have reached. Elisabeth's fears, it seems, were not unfounded.

Maurice Pryce, the British physicist, brushes aside such questions as philosophical, even metaphysical. He says that his "philosophy is to avoid philosophy," even though he realizes such a statement is itself philosophical. He regards as irrelevant all questioning of statistical descriptions of reality:

> I think there are certain questions of this kind which are grammatically acceptable questions, but meaningless in the physical context, and I suspect that this is one of them. . . . There are certain questions to which I can't get an answer because, in the context of what the physical world is, they have no real meaning. And some of the questions concerning actuality are, for me, questions of that type.

ONE day I walked along the Missouri River, close to the spot where Lewis and Clark wintered before they began their trek across the Rocky Mountains on their way to the Pacific. A replica of Fort Mandan is somewhat inaccurately but necessarily located on the flood plain of the great river about forty miles north of Bismarck. The actual site is now underwater, owing to the naturally shifting currents of the river. But the river's configuration has also been altered by the technological imposition of our idea of what a river is. Dams, made for leaching the river's power and frittering it away into an amusement park of electric can-openers and video games, impede by design the rush of effluent from high ground to low.

The river is much clearer now, a native tells me, than it ever was before the dams. The silt that used to churn from its depths is caught behind the concrete walls. The water I watch sliding past now is green like oxidized bronze, not brown and turgid as Lewis and Clark saw it.

Near the bank stabilized with stones where I walk, I can see water, wallowing and sucked into itself in spinning vortices. The solid-seeming surface, pocked and dimpled, changes itself at each moment. The content that is froth, battered against a stone at one moment, is swift, submerged current the next. Yet the froth remains, even as the current runs.

It is all a welter, this water. Made of molecules of wetness and of pattern.

Or is it a pattern? Can turbulence be mapped, or is it only turmoil, random and lawless? Are the tea-colored tatters of foam, left behind by the subaqueous forces hurling themselves against the stone embankment, merely the debris of design, the leftovers of what could not be contained in an equation of mass and velocity? The inevitable residue of chaos that clings to the underside of order?

We see this question most clearly in water, but it pervades the matter all about us. Water is simply swift where solids are slow. And its motion translucently apparent where the flux of air is invisible. But we are awash in a world of welter. We live, like fish, submerged in the bafflement of its motion.

Physicists call the phenomenon of turbulence—whether in water, smoke, or air currents—Brownian motion. They cannot predict in detail what shapes its constituent molecules will trace or the forces they will exert. Heraclitus was not speaking solely in metaphors when he said one never steps into the same stream twice. Both the content and the form of the stream are constantly changing. Only change *is* constant. We never watch the same flotilla of clouds moving down the sky, or the same refraction of rays in the sunset, nor see the same face twice.

The Missouri River, broad and muscled, has had much of its turbulence diffused by dams, although what will happen, once the cavity behind the dams silts up, is anybody's guess. Even that aspect of Brownian motion is beyond our reckoning. And what force is left to the Missouri it largely conceals beneath its patinaed skin.

BUT in the mountains the water from snowmelt pours down through rock-hardened arteries in a fury of white horses, leaping and spouting over boulders, crashing into a spray of crystal drops, purling smoothly and steadily over the lip of a rock, almost jellied in its constancy. Here, we can say, is the place where the water recoils on impact with the boulder and leaps. Here is where it turns to spray, hanging for a moment, forever, in the air. Here is where it becomes a solid, longitudinally ridged curve, spilling over the stone. The broad outline remains, the visual statistics of its motion, but the embodiment of that motion at each instant shifts, modulates, inflects, veers. Like the snowflake, which varies with the production of each six-pointed crystalline structure, liquefaction dissolves and emerges at each moment before our eyes.

Perhaps that is the reason we sit so long beside streams. They have the power to lure our minds, our perceptions, into their patterns. Our eyes cannot help drifting in the direction of the movement of the water, just as our ears cannot keep from following the movement of music.

We are swept into perceptual patterns of movement as if we ourselves were one of those crystal drops, rushing, merging, spinning, exploded upward. Only we are also able, at the same moment, to maintain our consciousness of the overall pattern. We apprehend, at those moments, not by analysis but by absorption. Even from the bank we do not observe but participate. Our minds run down the stream as fleet and fluid as water. Our perception following the movement becomes a part of it.

And the water itself exerts an influence over us. It does not lie there, inert of will. It does not say take me or leave me, just as you choose. It is neither apathetic nor coy. It murmurs, tugs, harangues, compels us. Put a human consciousness next to a waterfall, and it is instantly absorbed into its motion of infinite variety. We cannot but choose to look and look. Nor can we but choose to hear music *as* music. Not as single, unrelated sounds following one another sequentially.

What we call nature is not simply a matter of our choosing. There is a laboratory level on which physicists do choose their apparatus in accordance with what they choose to observe, and thus create, in a sense, phenomena. But it is not all a one-way street. There is also the strong, swift, seductive power of phenomena. The river pulls us into its depths as surely as it sucks the silt from the shoreline. The waterfall thunders imperious demands on our tympanic membrane. Music *makes* us follow.

We are dealing with substance here, not our own mere malleable whimsy. The potter presses his thumb inward and imposes a shape on his clay. But the clay, too, has its own reality. It has a definite resistance to the pressure of the hand. Who knows but what the clay does not itself demand a hand to shape it? We may push and prod protons into waves or particles, but they also push back. They make their own demands on the situation of which we are a part. They are at least as earnest as we are. It is indeed participation we are involved in here, not manipulation. A dance, not a puppet show. If you don't believe it, try jumping in the river.

We may indeed have consciously imposed our technological idea of what a river is on the Missouri; we may have cut into the muscle of the heartland here and implanted a series of pacemakers to regulate the arterial flow. But the river, soon or late, will make its own demands, will force our hand. We do not manipulate without consequences.

Seduction of another sort is at work here, too. It preys upon the mind that finds its mission ultimately futile, beyond its powers. It ends in the subtle corruption of the spy who at last capitulates and goes native.

Confronted with a current of faces drifting past, unaccountable, seen once and then receding in time and distance, confronted with a different face on the pillow, across the table, in the mirror each time he looks, the spy loses his nerve. It is too much; it is incomprehensible. The task overwhelms his faculties. He cannot keep up, can know neither himself nor his neighbors.

How can we love what falls through our fingers like water running, sand sifting? By the time we have targeted it, the target has flow. We miss the mark. Our acts fall to the ground, impotent.

The components of a system are too many, too fleet, too unpredictable for our analysis. The seduction is to despair.

In 1927 a colloquium of physicists met in Brussels to decide just what the limits of their capacities were. Einstein held out for embodiment, for a correspondence between reality and theory. But the pragmatists carried the day, claiming that quantum mechanics must instead satisfy itself with laws governing aggregates of events and states. For the first time scientists submitted to the notion that the world was too much for them to contemplate. They simply weren't up to it. It was physically impossible.

And who knows? Perhaps that capitulation was itself a necessary step. It certainly allowed quantum mechanics to advance at a more rapid pace, unhindered by the thorny questions that Professor Pryce studiously ignores.

But still, the questions nag. Those temperamentally disposed to pragmatism have no trouble sitting on the lid of Pandora's box. Einstein is dead. And as the discoverer of the quantum, Max Planck, himself pointed out, "A new scientific truth does not triumph by convincing its opponents and making them see the light, but rather because its opponents eventually die. . . ." Yet the lid keeps slipping, and every now and then some scientist, dissatisfied with pragmatism, lifts the lid a bit. Then the questions come pouring forth.

Can we really afford to contemplate anything *less* than the whole world, Brownian motion and all? Will the integrity of our own structure of consciousness allow us to stop at a mere statistical analysis, or is that an evasion of consciousness? Are the rewards that pragmatic physics provides through its ability to successfully manipulate matter alluring enough to seduce science from its primary course?

More is at stake here than the fate of invisible particles which you and I shall never see. Matter itself is at stake. The world. You and me. Consciousness. All meaning. All coherence. The cosmos itself. If individual particles are not significant, then neither are individual people, who are, after all, themselves phenomena.

In the sixth century Simplicius wrote a commentary on Aristotle's astronomy. He used the Greek phrase that translates literally "to save the phenomena," but which has been more frequently translated as "saving the appearances," primarily because our understanding of the term "phenomenon" has degenerated to mean something like "object" or "event." Owen Barfield explains, however, that the word actually "suggests neither wholly 'what is perceived, from within themselves, by men' nor wholly 'what, from without, forces itself on man's senses,' but something between the two." It is both our changing concept of the Missouri River and the river's undermining of those stabilized banks. It is both the pressure of the hand against the clay and the clay's own response to the pressure. That is the phenomena, the appearances.

Neither Aristotle, Simplicius, Barfield, nor I (and certainly not Plato or Heisenberg) would deny that beneath the phenomena lies a more fundamental truth about the world, one in which the thing-in-itself resides. But all temporal knowledge is necessarily phenomenal, of appearances. And just because it is a humbler sort of knowledge does not mean that it is invalid. Incarnation may be a descent from the eternal, but it is not an illusion.

"It would seem that the appearances are in danger," wrote Barfield, "and that they will require 'saving,' in a rather different sense of the term from that used of old by Simplicius . . . . The hypothesis of chance has already crept from the theory of evolution into the theory of the physical foundation of the earth itself. . . ." Historically, scientists developed a physical theory based on statistics at about the same time we gave our cultural assent to a science called sociology, also based on statistics. Both can provide us with a certain kind of data that can be used in predictions, whether of atomic decay or actuarial charts. But just as the spy is afflicted with a distinct uneasiness when the significance of a human life is defined by such aggregate data, so the minds of certain scientists are haunted by a restless dissatisfaction with such a physical reductionism.

The faces streaming by us on the sidewalk—how are they ever to become more than a smear across our vision? It goes beyond the power of human apprehension to attend to each one. Yet we know that, taken one by one, each face *can* be recognized, distinguished from all others. Love lights singly on each face passing the window, if it lights at all, and at the moment of recognition.

If our consciousness reaches the saturation point and refuses to absorb any more stimuli, if the faces do in fact begin to blur together, that is no vindication of the calculus of probability. It is simply an indication of our present perceptual limits. And if we must, for the time being, rely on a statistical interpretation of the universe, it is only because we have not yet developed the conceptual powers needed to recognize a further reality.

Pragmatism is essentially a conservative way of doing physics. It preserves what hard facts have been wrested from the welter and clings to them, gritting its teeth against the chaos that threatens to drown reason and *any* conception of the world along with it. But pragmatism never discovered, created, or conceived a single new theory, image, or vision. Not in physics, not in art, not in theology.

Pragmatists are content, for example, to ignore the implications of both relativity and quantum mechanics that show the observer to be inseparable from the system he is observing. How, indeed, can one maintain one's practical stance when the realm of observation keeps expanding outward in an ever-widening circle until it threatens to encompass all that there is—the universe and oneself with it?

"At this point, we are finally lost," says J. S. Bell.

> It is easy to imagine a state vector for the whole universe, quietly pursuing its linear evolution through all of time and containing somehow all possible worlds. But the usual interpretive axioms of quantum mechanics come into play only when the system interacts with something else, is "observed." For the universe there *is* nothing else, and quantum mechanics in its traditional form has simply nothing to say. It gives no way of, indeed no meaning in, picking out from the wave of possibility the single unique thread of history.

Bell ends by predicting that the quantum mechanical description must be finally superseded. He anticipates a new mode of perception involving "an imaginative leap that will astonish us." Such a leap is unlikely to be made by the pragmatists, however. And Bell acknowledges that so far his "view is that of a minority, but also that current interest in such questions is small. The typical physicist feels that they have long been answered, and that he will fully understand just how if ever he can spare twenty minutes to think about it."

The urge to attempt such an imaginative leap has something to do with what one means by the word "understand." What, after all, is the intent and purpose of consciousness itself? Heisenberg and Wolfgang Pauli had an early conversation about this when they were still students trying to comprehend Einstein's relativity theory. Pauli was satisfied that he understood a theory if he could construct a mathematical framework by which he could accurately predict the effects of an experiment. Heisenberg was not so sure. Ptolemy's cycles and epicycles had allowed the precise prediction of lunar and solar eclipses for fifteen hundred years. Yet Ptolemy did not really understand the planetary system. The two students finally agreed that understanding was a matter of having the necessary ideas and concepts to recognize that different phenomena are part of a coherent whole: "The ability to predict is often a consequence of understanding, of having the right concepts, but is not identical with understanding."

It took Einstein eleven years of unrelenting concentration

to produce the general theory of relativity, a concept that, as he pointed out, can now be easily grasped by any intelligent high school student. But the original *understanding* he described as a matter of anxious search and intense longing to wrest order from chaos.

Ironically, it is Heisenberg's own principles of indeterminacy that pragmatists cling to in their insistence that quantum mechanics is a closed system, that we will never go beyond it, never develop a new picture of phenomena. But Heisenberg himself was not a pragmatist; in fact, he might have been the twentieth century's most thoroughgoing Platonist. In his later years, like Einstein before him, he refused the limitations of seeing quantum mechanics as a closed system. Nor would he admit that lawlessness had the last word in physics, that a certain irreducible randomness was what made description necessarily vague. He confided to his friends that "though accident does play an important part in the subsequent emergence and development of a profusion of structures, it may well be that accident, too, is somehow related to the central order."

If Heisenberg hadn't been a physicist, he might have become a musician. In his memoirs he is as concerned to insist on the necessity of Schubert's B-Major Trio as he is on wave-function equations. He describes a Youth Assembly he attended at Prunn Castle in the Lower Altmuhl Valley in the spring of 1920. At that time German students were suffering from the physical and psychic dislocation brought on by the war. Europe as a structural concept had been shattered for them, and the effort of reconceptualizing society could only be borne, it seemed, by the youth of the country.

"I myself was much too unsure to join in the debates," Heisenberg says,

> but I listened and once again thought a great deal about the meaning of "order." From the remarks of the speakers it was clear that different orders, however sincerely held, could clash, and that the result was the very opposite of order. This, I felt, was only possible because all these types of order were partial, mere fragments that had split off from the central order; they

might not have lost their creative force, but they were no longer directed toward a unifying center. Its absence was brought home to me with increasingly painful intensity the longer I listened. I was suffering almost physically, but I was quite unable to discover a way toward the center through the thicket of conflicting opinions. . . . The talk was still going on when, quite suddenly, a young violinist appeared on a balcony above the courtyard. There was a hush as, high above us, he struck up the first great D minor chords of Bach's Chaconne. All at once, and with utter certainty, I had found my link with the center.

FINDING the "link with the center" has always been the task of the arts and sciences. And finding that link always means holding very tightly with one hand to the particular and groping with the other for that universal, encompassing, overwhelming central order.

"It is a good deal easier for most people to state an abstract idea than to describe and thus re-create some object that they actually see," Flannery O'Connor said of would-be writers. "They are concerned primarily with unfleshed ideas and emotions. . . . They are conscious of problems, not of people, of questions and issues, not of the texture of existence, of case histories and of everything that has a sociological smack, instead of with all those concrete details of life that make the actual mystery of our position on earth."

Han Cho, in twelfth-century China, made the same claims for the Oriental tradition of landscape painting as a link to the center. Its task was to display "the principle of organization connecting all things" through the precise perception of a single scene.

"But there's a certain grain of stupidity that the writer of fiction can hardly do without," O'Connor noted,

> and this is the quality of having to stare, of not getting the point at once. The longer you look at one object, the more of the world you see in it; and it's well to remember that the serious fiction writer always writes about the whole world, no matter how limited his particular scene. For him, the bomb

that was dropped on Hiroshima affects life on the Oconee River, and there's not anything he can do about it.

The link to the center is necessarily a particular event. Heisenberg, Han Cho, and O'Connor all knew this. All artists know it. Einstein knew it. That was why he refused to give up his insistence on "direct representation of physical reality," even though it evaded him in his own lifetime.

Spies: they are all after that elusive eddy, that bit of Brownian motion, the unpredictable vortex on the margin of the stream. Others may be content with the general drift, the statistically predictable current that makes it possible to get through their lives from one end to the other, ignoring or evading the demands of a reality that hounds us to our grave. But for the spy it is the so far—and perhaps forever—unpredictable, the lurking variables, the threat of whelming chaos that must be taken on: the mystery of things.

A calculated hodgepodge, an averaging of the odds, will not do. Taking that route, physicists turn into pragmatists; writers turn into reformers and moralists. "The way to despair is to refuse to have any kind of experience," O'Connor warned. And it is experience, embarrassing in its particularity, that statisticians refuse. The world, I suppose, needs moralists and reformers, even pragmatists. But it also needs those with a certain grain of stupidity who stare at things, who sit seemingly idle, too unsure to join in the debates, until they are suddenly and with utter certainty the link with the center.

Theoretical physics is becoming, undeniably, an exercise in aesthetics. Some have even claimed it as the art of the twentieth century. Its practitioners demand conceptual satisfaction from its structures. Like Keats, they believe that there is an ultimate equation in which truth and beauty define one another.

Indeed, if there is such a thing as truth, then it operates on many levels simultaneously. One area of truth does not have a solitary existence isolated from other regions of truth. Reality corresponds to itself, or, as Newton said, nature seems to have a remarkable property for self-similarity. And Murray Gell-Mann underscores this property by insisting that nature resembles itself at different levels:

> And that's probably what accounts for the possibility of using elegance as a criterion. We develop a mathematical formula, say, for describing something at a particular level, and then when we go to a deeper level we find that, in terms of mathematics, the equations at the deeper level are beautifully equivalent. Which means that we've found an appropriate formula.

But even now, those who are "science critics" the way Ruskin or Edmund Wilson were art critics sometimes fail to make the necessary connections, to see the correspondences.

"The scientist," Horace Freeland Judson has written, "enjoys the harsher discipline of what is and is not the case. It is he, rather than the painter or the poet in this century, who pursues in its stringent form the imitation of nature. . . . Here the scientist parts company with the artist. The insight must be sound. . . . The scientist is trying to get the thing right. The world is there."

Yet in the eighteenth century, it was Blake who was trying to get the thing right, realizing that Newton's inheritors of the Enlightenment were going at the world with a broadax, dismembering it like a violated corpse. No scientists in that age would have guessed that Blake's insight concerning the indivisibility of truth was sound. It took a century and a half and an Einstein to vindicate his rage against the "Atoms of Democritus and Newton's Particles of Light."

On the other hand, one can appreciate how Judson arrives at his devaluing of the truth in art today. "If to compare science to art seems—in the last quarter of this century—to undervalue what science does, that must be, at least partly, because we now expect art to do so little," he says.

> Before our century, everyone of course supposed that the artist imitates nature. Aristotle had said so; the idea was obvious, it had flourished and evolved for two thousand years; those who thought about it added that the artist imitated not just nature as it accidentally happens, but by penetrating to nature as it has to be. Yet today that describes the scientist.

In a spirit of charity he might have added that art was thrown off course *because* of a false aesthetics in science. (It is only very recently that scientists themselves have returned to Aristotle.) Reality being all of a piece may have disastrous as well as consoling implications. If science veers from its course, as it did during the Enlightenment, it drags art, religion, and the rest of human knowing in its wake.

If the art of our age is demonstrably weak and confused, that is not unrelated to scientists seeing stars as wallpaper. Art lost its nerve after Newton. It acquiesced in its isolation from Heisenberg's "central order." Writers refused to "write about the whole world," as O'Connor insisted they must. If they were cautious by nature, they settled for a slice of life. If they were more adventurous, they got sucked into the whirling maelstrom of Brownian motion.

And religion, too, lost its nerve. Ashamed of ecstasy, ashamed of scholastic rigor, ashamed of the very stars, it set its sights on wallpaper, taking its cue from pragmatists and positivists. Thus the conceptual crisis in physics is echoed by a conceptual crisis in religion. It gave up a three-storied universe as naive. It very nearly gave up God. And now, impoverished and impotent, it gropes toward that "imaginative leap that will astonish us."

*What is the difference between a cathedral
and a physics lab?
Are they not both saying Hello?*

—Annie Dillard

Chapter IX

In 1935 Einstein, along with his two assistants, Boris Podolsky and Nathan Rosen, contrived an experimental situation that would refute the claims that the quantum theory was a closed system, impervious to further clarification or refinement. Einstein had always refused to believe that the element of chance was inescapable in a physical description of the universe. He saw it as only a necessary stopgap until a better, more accurate model for matter could be devised. His own attempt at perfecting that model, his unified field theory, was never completed, but he did manage, with Podolsky and Rosen, to undermine the foundation of quantum theory—Heisenberg's principle of indeterminacy and the notion of statistical probability. These concepts were shown to be necessary but only intermediate steps in the continuing discovery of the world.

The challenge offered to quantum mechanics (now called the EPR effect after its inventors) was framed like this: Suppose there are two elementary particles—a pair of photons, say—that are in a combined state of interaction. While they are thus linked in a stable state, they must maintain equal and opposite spin numbers. (One particle must, for example, spin clockwise on its axis, its angular momentum pointing down, and the other must spin counter-clockwise and aim upward. The first, then, could be represented by the quantum number $\underline{S} = +\frac{1}{2}$, the other by $\underline{S} = -\frac{1}{2}$, preserving the symmetric value of zero.) The direction of the spin of one of the particles can be changed in an experiment using an electromagnet called a Stern-Gerlach device. The particle can be made to spin up or down, right or left, by changing the axis of this device. The other particle in the pair must then also change its direction in order to accommodate the necessary opposition. If the spin of its twin is altered up, it changes down; if to the left, then it changes to the right. Without introducing a distorting device into the situation, we can know with certainty what direction of spin the twin particle will take. This provides a way of measuring, contrary to Heisenberg, that is *not* indeterminate. Thus the wave function of the twin particle is shown to be not just a matter of statistical probability, but the real, factual situation.

This part of the EPR effect was profoundly satisfying to Einstein. But its further implications were just as profoundly disturbing.

Sometimes science validates itself by the very reluctance with which its disciples admit their findings. Max Planck, for example, had not *wanted* his experiments with the photoelectric effect to result in the discovery of the quanta. Quite the contrary. He had set up his experiment hoping to find that light came in continuous waves, not in discrete bundles of energy. He was personally distressed to find that it did. And Einstein, while he succeeded in torpedoing a very large hole in the supposedly self-contained system of quantum mechanics, at the same time uncovered another aspect of physical reality that he found equally abhorrent.

What the EPR effect inadvertently illustrated was that there is indeed some form of communication that occurs faster than the speed of light. For if the Stern-Gerlach device is shifted while the particles are flying away from one another, altering the direction of one of the photons, the other photon instantaneously "knows" about the change and also alters its direction. And the change occurs faster than light itself would be able to travel between the two, carrying any kind of signal to the split twin.

Physicists are constitutionally averse to using such words as "telepathy," but that was the only word Einstein himself could find to account for the result of his experiment. How else to explain the transmission of information faster than the speed of light?

Perhaps it was that very constitutional aversion that caused physicists to ignore the implications of the EPR effect for years afterward. It lay untouched while scientists went on with their work on the bomb, nuclear reactors, radiation therapy. It was not until the next generation of physicists came along that anyone paused to turn over this conundrum. Then in 1964 John S. Bell, intrigued by Einstein's abandoned legacy, worked out the mathematical proof for the EPR effect, producing Bell's theorem. And in 1972 the mathematical proof was experimentally verified in the Lawrence Berkeley Laboratory.

What quantum mechanics had supposedly taken away from physics several decades before—the correlation between cause and effect—was now given back, but on a much deeper and more awesome level. Classical mechanics had provided a mere dot-to-dot causal connection between objects. But now it was demonstrated that information somehow gets around faster than the fleetest photon. Such an effect even possibly accounts for the way some stars seem to explode, the whole body at once, without there being time for a "chain reaction" to travel from one part to another. Instead there is a simultaneous conflagration.

A variety of theories explain how and why the stars and the photons know these things. Perhaps the simplest is that there is indeed something beyond light, something physicists can only call superluminal connections, a net binding all the physical world into one knowing entity. According to this theory, reality is hierarchical and many-leveled. An unrelated, separate event—say, a single wave function—has a very low level of reality. But once a particle (wave) becomes correlated with another, that relationship is permanent, going on forever unless it is disrupted by some external force. Each new correlation in which it is involved lifts it to another and firmer level of reality. Single wave strands become braided together into a firmer and stauncher rope of substance. What were before only mathematical abstractions eventually become "real" things through multiplying correlations in somewhat the same way a random impression in the mind can be linked to other impressions, memories, and incidents, and eventually become something we call "thought." Through this network of physical correlations, the world is welded and wedded.

But this picture of ephemeral strands of wave functions being plaited, bit by bit, into substance may be starting at the wrong end of the tale. Or at least *in medias res*. For if the big bang theory of the emergence of the cosmos is correct, then all matter was in the beginning correlated in relationships of incredible density and still maintains a memory of that initial intimacy. If the modern mind finds it difficult to imagine the human race springing from the archetypal parents, Adam and Eve, let it ponder its aboriginal kinship with the matter that now makes up Mars and Arcturus.

Another possible way of explaining the EPR effect is by its very nature incapable of proof. This explanation relies on such a thoroughgoing determinism that in the end it makes science itself a futility. It relies on the logical possibility that we only delude ourselves when we think the lab technician makes a *choice* about changing the axis of the Stern-Gerlach device. We assume he *could* have chosen to change it to the left rather than the right or to down rather than up. But perhaps the choice does not really exist. Perhaps his own actions are themselves governed by some even greater Stern-Gerlach device. Perhaps it is not he who controls the spin of the photon but he who is controlled. In such a case there is simply nothing more to be said.

Human beings seem to have a constitutional need to see the rest of the world as obeying inexorable physical laws. But to see ourselves in such a plight unnerves us. If flipping the switch is no more a matter of choice than the photon's maintaining an opposite and equal spin in relation to its twin, then physics—and indeed all human endeavor—is a game we don't care to play anymore.

But of course we do go on playing, even in the teeth of such a possibility. And if the situation is incapable of logical proof one way or the other, perhaps it is aesthetic proof we must finally rely on to convince ourselves that we do control the switch. For the patterns the rest of the world makes are simple, pure, and beautiful. All the photon's paths are righteousness. The symmetry of spin velocities is a primal example. But our own intrusion into the pattern is most often confused, distorted, and awkward. If we were a part of a compelling pattern, at least in the same way that photons are, the tracery of our acts would be infinitely more elegant than it is. The internal evidence of the pattern itself convicts us. We do not fit.

Indeed, it is a mystery why we should admire, even desire with a good deal of passion, the pattern we observe the world taking, while we ourselves are at once both proud and wistful about our own exclusion from the beauty and unity of the cosmos. Proud because our exclusion means that we are not bound to obedience in the manner of photons. Wistful because our exclusion makes us the ugly ducklings of the universe, the misfits in matter.

Our very inability to choose those paths that make for harmony inside the boundaries of our own bodies testifies to the fatal nature of our freedom. We eat, drink, inhale our own damnation. Our self-abuse is limited only by the means we can find at hand to destroy ourselves. And the inability of the individual person to nurture health inside his own human housing is multiplied geometrically in conglomerates of his kind. What we think of today as the most advanced civilizations in history are those that offer the most varied panoply of poisons to its citizens. All its products, from automobiles to fuel wastes, turn out to be weapons turned against itself. It is as though there were a blind desire for death buried in each of us. Even the achievements of our best and brightest, from Einstein to Sakharov, are turned against the entire race. Given a choice, we cannot but choose death. We live, indeed, in bodies of death. We are the death-stars of the cosmos, subjugating our very cells and molecular structures to insupportable stresses till they warp and buckle.

Suppose that the world is one tissue, never erring, always internally consistent. Suppose that this obedience is, as David Bohm has explained the EPR effect, *implicit*, embedded in all matter, the laws governing its nature written on its heart. Is this not the creation that God called very good on the sixth day?

Then how wide the gulf between ourselves and the universe. Far from knowing our parts perfectly, we hardly know what to do from one moment to the next. Our proper path is obscure to the keenest eye. Our explicit knowledge, the things we can speak aloud or write down and think about, is always partial and circumstantial; we despair of the kind of implicit knowledge that sustains the rest of the world. We cannot even afford to let our right hand know what the left is doing, lest we spoil what meager grace is granted us.

No wonder Max Planck, the only avowed Christian among those European physicists working on re-conceiving the world in the early part of the century, was forced to divorce what he called objective truth from subjective truth in order to maintain his balance and his faith. How else to explain the rightness of the cosmos and the crookedness of man? And today we still rely on this theological crutch to explain our awkward position to a dubious or disinterested world.

Of two minds, we speak about the world of matter and the world of the spirit. The inner and the outer realities. Science and religion. Two separate truths.

But can truth ever be anything but one and remain the truth? As Wolfgang Pauli pointed out to his friend Heisenberg, division is an attribute of the devil.

Those who place their faith in what they call "objective truth" ignore the fact that they *create* the objects, the phenomena, out of undifferentiated being through their own consciousness. And those who are polarized to "subjective truth" submit to a schizophrenia that denies the very dust from which they are made. In their zeal for spirit, they make matter their enemy and thus become self-despisers.

Heisenberg saw the flaw in Planck's embattled theology. He saw that if there were such a thing as truth, it must be one. There are not scientific and religious truths, to be stored on separate shelves of the mind and taken out and used as occasion demands. Truth is not a tool; it is the one who makes demands. "Admittedly," he says, the subjective realm of an individual, no less than a nation, may sometimes be in a state of confusion. Demons can be let loose and do a great deal of mischief, or, to put it more scientifically, partial orders that have split away from the central order, or do not fit into it, may have taken over. But in the final analysis, the central order, or the "one" as it used to be called and with which we commune in the language of religion, must win out. . . . It is in this context that my idea of truth impinges on the reality of religious experience. I feel that this link has become much more obvious since we have understood quantum theory.

Heisenberg is not trying to prove the existence of God here in the same way that Aquinas did. In fact, he recognizes that "proof" of anything, even physical laws, is no longer possible in the way that the eighteenth-century rationalists envisioned it. We can muster a fairly plausible mythology for matter and the way it works on one level of reality, only to discover that the story has to be recast on the next level. The best we can do is to say that the world is analogous to itself, internally consistent, resembles itself on multiple levels.

It was in fact because the modern sensibility despaired of proving anything at all that it was driven to split the world into objective and subjective realms. And subjectivity became the haven, or rather the closet, for that which cannot be proved but which we know somehow it is madness to give up. We have made an uneasy truce between the two realms for generations now. People line up on one side of the barricade or the other according to their occupation or temperament.

But now the worst fears of both sides are being confirmed. Those who relied on inner truth, a superior kind more rarefied than that governing common creation, must now face the fact that their very thoughts are themselves physical events, exchanges of energy on an admittedly high level of complexity, but still embarrassingly material.

And on the other side, those who would reduce those energy exchanges to a series of levers and cogs, dumbly pushing and pulling the universe through its random course, must now see that the world of phenomena depends on us. It's no good insisting on the superior reality of tables and chairs, sticks and stones, bricks and bats. There are no such things, no objects, without a consciousness to conceive them as such. Not only that, but the cogs and levers are not, after all, deaf and dumb and conquerable. They are not even really cogs and levers, but droplets of intelligence, agile and quick, murmuring to one another through means both expansive and intimate.

If I have truth in me,
it will break out one day.
I cannot repel it:
my own self I'd repel.

—Karol Wojtyla

Chapter X

FOR days after I first read about the Einstein-Podolsky-Rosen experiment and its subsequent validation, I seethed and raved. I dreamed a thousand dreams full of stars and voices. I had no idea why. My reaction was as outlandish and riddled to me as it was to others. I only knew the sown seed, covered over in the dark, was swelling. This unspeakable sort of knowledge that sprouts and grows while we sleep and rise, night and day, we know not how, is perhaps itself part of the implicit nature of the cosmos. It may be our last remaining link to our kinship with the knowing photon that carries its kenning so lightly. Since we are, like it or not, composed of muddy matter ourselves, perhaps our molecules, if nothing else, struggle to push us in the right direction. They do, after all, have a lot to lose by having wandered into the peculiar constellation of electromagnetic fields we call ourselves.

At any rate, the biologist Michael Polanyi has labored to describe for his fellow scientists the bedrock of what he calls the "tacit dimension" of human consciousness, an underlying knowledge so taken for granted, so obvious as to have become invisible to us.

Say that one is a zoologist doing research on the nervous system of a frog. Before the relationships that make up such a system may be put into formulas that can be passed around among one's colleagues and mutually considered, the frog must first be tacitly recognized as an entity in itself. This is the sort of *a priori* knowledge, the goes-without-saying assumption from which all scientific or objective investigation proceeds. Even the act of applying a description, whether in words or in mathematical symbols, to a subject is itself a tacit assumption that the two entities can be meaningfully related. Polanyi emphasizes the importance of discovering the obvious:

We are approaching here a crucial question. The declared aim of modern science is to establish a strictly detached, objective knowledge. . . . But suppose that tacit thought forms an indispensable part of all knowledge, then the ideal of eliminating all personal elements of knowledge would, in effect, aim at the destruction of all knowledge. The ideal of exact science would turn out to be fundamentally misleading and possibly a source of devastating fallacies.

In other words, "we know things, and important things, that we cannot tell." How can we explain, for instance, that the frog *is* a frog to begin with? Or even a "thing"?

Whatever statement we may devise about reality, there is always a wordless, immediate fathoming that precedes it. Built into us, a part of our very structure of consciousness, is a means of real-izing the world, of detecting and verifying its existence. By the time we get around to formulating that reality in words or mathematical symbols, we have already forgotten that initial confrontation with the frog, that moment when it coalesced out of the burr and glint of ricocheting photons bombarding our retinas as a thing to be reckoned with. In less than a tenth of a second we are already so busy analyzing it and thinking *about* it that we discount and even forget the antiphonal element of our knowledge, that spontaneous apprehension that has, by the very nature of its suddenness, the quality of revelation.

To illustrate this enigma of tacit knowledge, Polanyi uses the paradox contained in Plato's *Meno*: "To search for the solution of a problem is an absurdity; for either you know what you are looking for, and then there is no problem; or you do not know what you are looking for, and then you cannot expect to find anything." Our difficulty with comprehending this paradox is that we equate knowing with being able to formulate. But there is also a kind of knowledge—that which Polanyi calls tacit—embedded in us, just as it is embedded in elementary particles. It is a part of our very structure. To eliminate it would be to unmake ourselves.

We must somehow already know truth in order to recognize truth when we see it, even when we cannot name it.

And the only way the researcher has of knowing when he has found the solution to the problem is by having some intimation of it hidden in himself. Suddenly, out of the welter of particulars swirling in his mind, the answer congeals, comes together, fits. He knows it is the proper solution only by the sense of satisfaction in himself that coherence brings. He must, in a sense, and in some part of himself, know the answer in order to recognize it when he sees it. It is all a matter of bringing it into focus, of disclosing to himself the truth already latent within him.

To say this is to say no more than both the saints Paul and Augustine have also said. Paul claimed that the Gentiles do "by nature what the law requires," that it is, in fact, "written on their hearts." The truth appropriate to a human's being is encoded in that being, however blind or deaf he may be to the message it carries. It is not something added on, like a lean-to tacked on to the main edifice of the mind; but like the chromosomes, whose very arrangement of molecules *is* the organism's essential information, its code for the business it's about, we bear in our bodies the information we need in order to be.

"Truth! Truth! How the very marrow of my soul within me yearned for it," cries Augustine, one of those Gentiles Paul vouched for. "Unless we had some sure knowledge of it, we should not desire it with such certainty." And that knowledge comes "by means of the image within us." The African calls his own being "a trace of the single unseen Being from whom it was derived." We are smudges, hieroglyphics, notes to one another about being.

We know truth when we find it because it is already within us. All creation is internally consistent, true to the nature of the one who made it, not really *ex nihilo*, but out of himself. Just as it dwells within every region and relationship of the cosmos, it dwells within us. It is not the truth that is absent from us, Augustine insists, but we who are absent from ourselves, where the truth has been pleased to dwell. "You were within me, and I was in the world outside myself."

The world outside himself is the alien land the spy wanders, infiltrates with his presence. It is a world where all men have forgotten who they are because they are all vagrant, absent from themselves. Their deserted selves continue to propel their incubi through space, to go to work, go home, go in and out, to and fro upon the face of the earth. There is indeed in this alien land a great deal of going, of clatter and rush, and very little stealth and sitting still. All the tasks that demand immobility and stalking are gone. We are no longer hunters or fishermen. We have no spinners or hermits. Even the Trappists talk now. It is only the spy, disguised and double-lived, whose eye is single, like a needle's.

He is trying to discover, to spy out what it is he already knows. He goes to Carthage or to Kentucky, joins the Manichees or the Moonies. With any luck he lands in prison, where he is at last forced to sit still. Even Augustine ended in a prison of sorts—the Church. His ordination at Hippo was more like an arrest and a sentence to lifetime incarceration. He was kidnapped and dragged before the bishop, weeping and protesting. And like any prisoner, he brought with him only the clothes he stood up in. Thus lightened, the prisoner, the spy, stumbles against that hidden reality he has been stalking.

But the African saint had a means at his disposal that has been missing from our world for centuries now. It was called anagogical vision, a way of seeing multi-layered reality whole. Flannery O'Connor called it "an attitude toward all of creation, and a way of reading nature which included the most possibilities," one of those possibilities being the Divine life and our participation in it. For Augustine the Scriptures were not *either* a matter of fact *or* of symbol. They were both simultaneously. Metaphor was not a mere ornament added to meaning but the point where mind and matter converged.

And now I, too, had a way of reading nature that included the most possibilities. It included, for one thing, the permeation of nature with the possibility of consciousness. It included the permeation of myself with tacit knowledge. The revelation that matter itself was more than we had dreamed for centuries, that it called and responded in ways we had denied in our ignorant arrogance, that day poured forth speech to day, and night declared knowledge to night, that their words were heard to the ends of the world—all this wedded the world for me once more.

One did not need to sneak from assignations with rocks and river mud to a filmy world of insubstantial spirit like a bigamist, faithful now to one side, now to the other of his divided understanding. The supposedly dead world was resurrected. It came alive again in my consciousness, just as Christ himself is resurrected and comes alive in each believer's heart where he has lain, a dormant, dry seed, in the darkened understanding.

I do not think that this is too much to say. Indeed, I believe we all *do* say it each time we link heaven and earth in the prayer we have been commanded to pray, or when we repeat the Apostles' Creed, stitching ourselves to God by means of his Incarnation, the diving Christ who splits the waters of chaos to dredge from its convulsions the fetid refuse of creation determined to unmake itself.

If you want to recover the psalms, to see the hills leap and the trees clap, to hear the stars and stones shout, you have to be a spy. This is the only contemplative mode left to our impoverished age. To ring bells and go barefoot is self-indulgent, and would only call attention to yourself and distract the concentration. No, you have to be a spy, sensing the presence of what is hidden, listening in to the voices echoing through the infinite lines of the cosmos.

We sit and stare at tulips. We hear the day pouring forth its speech, its very photons wise with embedded righteousness. This is the spy's quarry: God manifest. The Incarnation. The clues pointing to the coherence that holds the universe together. The discovery of what we already know, what dwells within and among us. The recovery of sight for the blind.

The world is there, as Judson, the science critic, points out. And, adds Paul, the saint, what can be known about God, his invisible nature, can be clearly perceived in that world. The world is there, and its truth is indivisible. It resists our falseness by breaking our shoddy constructions against its substance and potency. But its truth, to be apprehended, demands an answering and indivisible truth in ourselves. If we are indeed blind, or at best seeing through a glass darkly, if we are, as Augustine said, absent from ourselves so that the knowledge that indwells in us is useless, then what can deliver us from our own incubus, our body of death?

Paul again answers us. If we cannot know with the same kind of completeness of the cosmos, then we must rely on being known.

Let yet another prisoner, this time the Russian Solzhenitsyn, testify to the experience of "being known":

> I had learned in my years of imprisonment to sense that guiding hand, to glimpse that bright meaning beyond and above myself and my wishes. I had not always been quick to understand the sudden upsets in my life, and often, out of bodily and spiritual weakness, had seen in them the very opposite of their true meaning and their far-off purpose. Later the true significance of what had happened would inevitably become clear to me, and I would be numb with surprise.

Whatever we can know, however we can sense the presence of a hidden reality, it is because we have already been known, been created. Our tacit knowledge, the truth of our lives, was shaped before we were knit together in our mother's womb, made in secret, intricately wrought in the depths of the earth.

There is much more information zinging around the world than we are ordinarily aware of, and it makes use of channels no cyberneticist has yet discovered. Sharks strike, at the last moment, by locating their prey through sensing the bioelectrical fields that surround living bodies. Twins, separated from birth, grieve simultaneously and give the same names to their children. Schools of fish wheel on some constantly shifting consensual axis, and flocks of birds rise as one body to some synchronic signal.

And, like birds, ideas are suddenly "in the air," springing up, spreading faster than fire. In 1925 three people, working independently of one another, discovered quantum mechanics.

It seems like birds and fish and photons find it easy to let themselves be known, be thought into existence. Perhaps that's the secret of their success. And even our ideas are better than our selves. Polanyi points out that the invisible structure we call science is maintained in its integrity because of the weight each scientist exerts on the enterprise, a weight sufficient to hold it together in a unified tradition. It sustains this coherence from one generation to another, across political boundaries, in spite of disparate disciplines.

We can, it seems, be the universe knowing itself, can know everything, except ourselves. That bright meaning beyond and above ourselves belongs to some other being, from whom it must be wrested, and who disguises himself, leaving us numb with surprise when we finally catch him. The crafty Jacob jumped a man beside the road and got a new name: Israel, "He-Struggles-with-God." He was on his way home to Esau, his estranged twin.

Even after the dissolution of the elements
in which it existed from the beginning,
the soul, like a guardian of what is its own,
remains in them and,
even when it is mingled with the general
*   mass,*
it does not give up its individuality
in the subtlety and mobility
of its intellectual power.
It does not deviate
in the delicate diffusion of the elements,
but joins the mass with its own constituents,
and, having gone along with them,
when they are poured back into the universe,
it remains in them always,
wherever or however nature arranges them.

—Gregory of Nyssa

Chapter XI

WHAT is this wind we go hunting like spoor-scenting wolves, hungry for the blood at the world's source? What, after all, *is* spirit? When I go on at such lengths about consciousness, a word suspiciously shared with the Hare Krishnas and a catalogue chock-full of other consciousness-enhancing sects, am I really talking about spirit? Or is this just old-time religion replated with a thin veneer of respectable scientism?

There is a way of talking about consciousness and that organ of the body we call the brain as if they were two distinct entities. Is there the life of matter and the senses on the one hand, and the life of the spirit on the other? Or is there only life? Is there one dance, the one between consciousness and matter, or are there two or even three? But if there are three—or a thousand—don't they, touching at any point, become one? One immense, eternally unfolding, multifoliate shape of being?

If consciousness remains unlocatable in the brain, if it refuses to be pinned down to a point as other functions are, does that mean it has another, totally different kind of existence? That it can be divorced from matter, that it can eventually, with training, spurn its carnal footing and float free? Will some highly disciplined jogger, one fine morning, experience the rapture in which his fully attuned consciousness drifts free of his dilated arteries and secreting sweat glands?

Physiologically, the cord is not so easily cut. Consciousness is indeed elusive of location, but it does depend for its operation on the electrical energy generated in the brain's cells. If certain chemical structures are allowed into the higher brain stem—alcohol or morphine, for instance—they set up barricades to block the energy produced there. One stumbles, faints, falls, is out like a light. Consciousness, if it continues to exist, at least can no longer communicate with or through the body. And the body, left to itself, cannot carry on for long.

The separation, the disjunction, then, between mind and body is only a contrivance of conceptualizing. A device to make talking about the phenomenon possible. We can't have one, at least not for long, without the other, any more than we can have a coin with only one side or a cup with an interior but no exterior.

But words are such small, light things. "Mind" and "body." Only four letters each. We set them down on opposite sides of the paper, draw a line between them as a barrier, and there you are. There I am. There the human condition is. Two separate natures. The oldest and easiest trick in the world. "Give the mind two seconds alone and it thinks it's Pythagoras," says Annie Dillard. Drawing lines in the air, carving up reality.

But wait. We're not done with this quite yet. Consciousness is supposedly a rather late development in the history of the universe. Creation or evolution—whichever story you take, it makes very little difference. If you start with light (which both stories do) and end with us (which they also both do), there's quite a bit of stuff in the cosmos before you come to consciousness: chemical elements, both noble and so unstable they tremble their substance away in gamma rays before you can blink; gases; rocks; water; dirt. We won't even worry about what we call living things.

Animate and inanimate. Souled and unsouled. It's one thing to say my dog has a certain dim consciousness and quite another to say that the scoria, the piece of red clinker I picked up in the North Dakota badlands, a by-product of the smelting that goes on in lightning-ignited lignite, has any part in consciousness. Plants may have certain preferences for music and other nurturing variables in their environments. But who would make the same claim for a clinker?

On the other hand, where *is* the line, Pythagoras, between the quick and the dead? Does it really lie between stones and stonecrop? "Clearly, a molecule of carbon dioxide that crosses a cell boundary into a leaf does not suddenly 'come alive,'"

David Bohm points out, "nor does a molecule of oxygen suddenly 'die' when it is released to the atmosphere. Rather, life itself has to be regarded as belonging in some sense to a totality, including plant and environment."

The body I am today came yesterday in a crate of avocados from California. India spins in my tea-drenched blood this morning. Minerals dissolved for millennia in a subterranean aquifer irrigate my interior, passing through the portals of my cell walls, which are themselves filigrees of chemical construction. I am really only a river of dissolute stones, the wash of world-water dammed for a melting moment in the space I call my body, some of it ceaselessly brimming over the spillway and flowing on down drains, into other tributaries, catching in some other body's pond, until one day the whole structure cracks and buckles, giving up in one great gush its reservoir of mineraled water.

We soluble stones do indeed give voice to the universal longings of creation: we open our throats and bleat "Hosanna!" and "Blessed be he!" But if this flitch of flesh *should* fail, the very stones, the naked, unelaborated grit itself would cry out. I find some comfort in that. Nevertheless, when the son of man comes, will he find faith on earth? The earth itself is more faithful than what I have hoarded of it within my own sensible skin.

Still, our niche, our place, is to give voice to the cry. The stones must cry only if we fail, if faith can be found nowhere else. This is our big chance. To stand, slung upright and outward from the surface of this earthstone still bubbling like a crucible beneath our feet, and shout toward stars dead and dispersed but still shining into our eyes: "Hello out there. Hosanna!" Or to listen along the pounding veins, vessels, and caves of our blood for the beat of the song by which to tune our tempers. This is our chance to be choirmaster of creation. Morning star, on the parsec, please. And earthworms, enter with a certain dark tremolo.

Are we making too much of matter? The concrete calliope and its configurations of sound have absorbed us, but the wind pumping through its bellows is still eluding us.

Very well. Let us continue stalking our prey; perhaps we can come at it by indirection and stealth. We will not talk about spirit just yet. We will instead follow the riverbed of world-water further upstream, for, according to Paul, what *can* be known about God is in plain sight, "clearly perceived in the things that have been made," the invisible leaving clues in stark-staring creation.

Then why aren't more theologians biologists, more oceanographers astronomers? Jonathan Edwards, who studied spiders, was a rarity. Most often it is the scientists who attempt theology. Newton wrote commentaries on Daniel and Revelation. Kepler avowed geometry was God, so great was his awe of the bare beauty of perfect forms. And some of Einstein's cohorts had to plead with him to stop going on so about God. But the battle Augustine fought in the fourth century to reclaim from its reduction to evil "matter completely without form and quality, out of which are formed the qualities we perceive," is scarcely chronicled today by those concerned for an unsteady coalition of a nebulous spirit and a statistical society.

Perhaps we were thrown off the scent a long time ago, and still are, because spiritualists strike us as being cut from finer cloth, as having subtler sensibilities. Yet the Manichees whom Augustine battled were, strange to say, great gluttons. They sat about, sweating and stinking in order to show their disdain for the flesh, and stuffed their craws with huge quantities of food brought by their disciples, so that they might transmogrify the matter there into a more rarefied element by virtue of its having passed through their ethereal entrails. Indeed, they found it their solemn, religious duty to salvage as much of the world as they could swallow. Far from giving thanks to God for good creation, as the apostle describes our proper task, they made it their business to despise this palpable world, even as its juices ran down their chops.

Such a perversion of consciousness makes us tisk. But we too have heretics sufficient unto our day. Unfortunately, heretics are often so well-intentioned that one doesn't like to puncture the heretical balloons. Such balloons as appear regularly in devotional books, clever, succinct, expressed thus: "Love people, not things."

Now there is certainly no biblical precedent for such a gnostic notion. We are told that God values human beings more than sparrows (and, by implication, more than the lilies of the field). But that does not mean that sparrows and field flowers are valueless and should not be loved. Or that people are not things. Our thinghood is every bit as thoroughgoing as that of birds and flowers. When we *eat* the birds and the flowers, an everyday occurrence, we absorb their very molecules into our own cells. Thus what was once a sparrow becomes a thumb, and a lily turns into a tooth.

Let us not be so high-handed about matter. Such small confusions grow into mighty heresies. It is only one such small well-intentioned step from despising our thinghood to despising the ragged wounds that redeem the world.

The question that we ponder, therefore, as we crouch in the cleft of the rock, waiting for the wind to come up, is this: how much does matter matter?

Gnostics, of any ilk or century, say not at all. Only spirit matters. From Manichees to mathematicians, they all show a distinct disregard for the universe that is snuggling up to them at every joint, in every crevice and orifice of their bodies. It fills the spaces between their fingers, wraps every eyelash, but they remain indifferent. Their mind's eye is single, fixed on a vanishing point. No pictures, Dirac warned Schrödinger, no models. Just so the religious Gnostics piled posited world upon world, each one more immaterial as it receded from our own coarse, slovenly one, until, in a final quantum leap, they spanned the abyss that separates matter from spirit.

They would have served their cause better by not imagining such a thing. For as soon as it is touched by the groping, grubby imagination, spirit does become a thing. We can only imagine things, rather than no-things.

Only God himself remains finally unimaginable, a fact that also makes us a little petulant at times, but there you are. He gives us clues, as Paul confessed. Light, energy, the yellow iris sitting in perfect, self-contained being on my table, its petals a complete double-trinitarian story: three pent inward, three arching out. They tell with truth "what can be known about God." They do not, cannot lie. But they tell only what can be known, not all that there is. Still, the clues we *can* know, can find lying about, are what summon us, haunt and herd us into the presence of that which overwhelms and incinerates our senses.

What *can* be known is my proper business. And the kinds of creatures humans are can know, comprehend, understand only through the senses, and the senses can know only matter.

Carl Sagan's comment on a television documentary about the brain, that mind is "only" physiological, betrays our culture's common anti-sacramental assumptions. The consensus is that all religion is at bottom gnostic, based on a special gnosis, not on creation. One sees it in Sagan's studied secularism, but also in the moralistic injunction to love people, not things. As though we were not made of the same dust as our dogs. One sees it in the way contemporary scholars give up in despair the task of trying to neatly put the terms the Hebrews used for "spirit" into modern categories: "one would be tempted to make a distinction by calling *ruach* the whole non-physical aspect of man were it not that it is difficult to say that the Hebrews did not conceive both *ruach* and *nephesh* as in some way physical and having substance, *modern notions of immateriality being beyond them*"(A Theological Wordbook of the Bible, Macmillan, 1950, p. 144, emphasis added).

What we want, it seems, when we talk about our spirit in a way that implies that which can pass through the sieve that sifts out the grosser aspects of our being, is to affirm the potency of the invisible. To be sure, there is a certain smugness in the scientific tone when it speaks of "mere" mind, as though it had escaped the necessity of acknowledging anything more than mere, anything like mystery.

But if what we want is to affirm invisible powers, we have to go no further than our own molecules. Made up of atoms, made up of invisible electrical charges around a nucleus, made up of baryons, made up of quarks. And by the time we get to the quarks, the physicists, who long ago left visibility behind, feel they have passed beyond the realm of reality. No individual quarks have ever been observed by any method; they have only been mathematically posited. We know that they, like unicorns, somehow *ought*, aesthetically, to be there. The balance of the universe is poised on their existence. The abstract mathematics is real; the pattern, the scheme that insists on their necessity to the elegance and coherence of the cosmos, is there. Yet the "body" of a proton is supposedly made up of three quarks, each of whose rest mass would greatly exceed that of the proton they compose. But almost all their substance is, at least in this story, poured out into the energy necessary to bind the bit together. Hence their identity as particles evaporates into energy of a force so great that it is beyond current comprehension. Thus by far the largest "part"—if one can talk in terms so crude when describing something so ephemeral—of matter is actually an invisible binding force.

This is your body we're talking about. This is matter. As immaterial as the most rarefied scholar's spirit. Who now dares scoff at the Hebrew's *ruach* and *nephesh*, the substantial spirit, the life-breath shared with all living things? How is "spirit" to be defined at all in a way that will cleave it from the bones of Creation? What is physical and what is non-physical? Isn't any *thing* physical, even the diaphanous tissue of thought? How did we ever fall into this heretical habit of despising creation, of disembodying our spirits and disemboweling the world? Where did we pick up the trick of speaking of a thin spiritual dimension to life as though it were a layer of ozone hovering just over the heavier, more vulgar oxygen, as if it were not pouring and pounding through every stream of blood, every column of sap, penetrating the very stones themselves?

Well—from the Greeks, perhaps, those picadors of the universe, who started the penchant for categorizing, for drawing lines in the air. But not from Paul, although his thoroughly

Hebrew soul may have found itself accommodating the sophisticated Greeks with their modern notions of immateriality somewhat more than he had intended. When he speaks disparagingly of flesh, it is flesh that refuses to recognize the source of its life, that denies the destination of its own consciousness, that sees itself, satanically, as self-sufficient. But it was no Gnostic, no matter-demeaning Manichee who asked in amazement, "Do you not know that your *bodies* are members of Christ?"

Flesh that does not know itself to be quickened by Christ is a fetid sore, a cancer on the cosmos. It is God's life that flows through the arteries of the world, that seeps in the capillaries enclosing each quark, that sustains being at every moment. For what life is there apart from the Creator's? Gregory of Nyssa claimed that "the divine is equally present in all things, and, in like manner, it pervades all creation and it does not exist separated from being, but the divine nature touches each element of being with equal honor, encompassing all things within itself." In which case, not loving things comes very near to despising God.

There is only one fountain filled with blood, the world's blood, from which flows all the life there is. There are no separate drinking fountains for butterflies and Brahma bulls, for Krishnas and Christians. We may find it very tasteless of the Creator, but he pours out life indiscriminately, with the abandon of a drunken host at the feast. The sun shines on the just and the unjust; he shows mercy to whom he will. It galls us, but he goes right ahead.

For us, the only line is the one between the created and the uncreated, and that is a sheer cliff. Hang there he who dares. We can have nothing to do with the uncreated, except to suppose that that is where God takes a rest from us. All the rest, all being—spirit, matter, consciousness, call it what you will—is creation. What we name our spirits were called forth, shaped out of chaos, as surely as our bodies, and all kept churning and gyring and winking and chirping by God's own life poured into them.

Even flesh—the sour, stagnant pools of being that refuse to

recognize and rejoice in this flood of life, that attempt to frustrate the gush of grace—even that sucks whatever being it allows itself from the source it denies.

And still the mute mountains, the dumb desert, the dying stars wait for us to provide a throat for their thanksgiving.

There must be a great logjam in the cosmos. One can almost hear it groaning and creaking some summer nights, threatening to give way under the pressure of pent-up praise. Its little baryons and mesons and leptons are thrumming away in such harmonic obedience to their design that one's own destiny-defying body can feel, take ignorant comfort in the bone-deep drone.

Thoreau said he went to the woods to drive nature into a corner. But of course there is no corner to drive it into, save the vortex of our own consciousness. All the sad suburbanites make their treks to trees and hills and ponds in shells they call Marauder and Prowler and Apache. Perhaps they are just as fierce as Thoreau in his intentions.

I go stumping around like a scarecrow, not knowing what in the world I'm doing nor what the world's doing in me as it gestates in the cavern of my cranium, lacing my brain with enigmatic engrams. I have no more idea of how to corner nature in my consciousness than of how to fly. If anyone's cornered, it's me, skewered and shaken like a stupefied Saint Sebastian, lolling and lunatic. I don't know *how* to do it, how to drive, herd, badger, corral the world; but when it happens I know.

In my part of the country there are many plants that the field guides describe as "armed." Prickly pear and pincushion cactus, wild thorny gooseberries and Spanish dagger that prick and slash the unwary. The ground itself is rocky and hard. Lewis and Clark's corps of discovery could scarcely make their footsore way across it, and nearly starved to death from lack of game before they made it across to the fertile northwestern river valleys. They claimed that even their Indian guides were so hungry that when a rare hapless deer was killed, they pulled the entrails from its slit belly still smoking and devoured them immediately, contents and all.

Yet what I know when I lie on a boulder that clenches the day's store of sunlight in its granite fist is trust. I do not trust it to love, shelter, or care for me. I have seen an avalanche that the shoulder of a mountain shrugged into angles so vertiginous that one grew dizzy standing among the slanting, upheaved gobbets, trees pointing in impossible directions, staring into root-webs cast up and earth cracks that could swallow a horse. God may love me more than the sparrows, but this soil has a heart of stone for humans.

But I declare I know trust when I lie down on this rock. I trust it to *be* what it is. Stones are for breaking; they are to resist. And they are true to their own nature, with no swerving or deception. There is not another of my kind, no matter how beloved, I can trust for that. In fact, every ounce of integrity wrested from that deceptive entity we call "human" nature is held up as a deep-delved jewel for our acclaim. We admire a man for finishing a difficult mission, for being true to a task, but we never think of praising a rock for being hard and impervious, or water for being wet.

This trust we have for nature is the source of what we so crassly call relaxation and recreation. We can relax because we know the mountain will not give way like papier-maché beneath us; the sea is not a sham but salty and earnestly implacable; the desert, for all its dangerous mirages, does not deceive. The earth's violence is not a stunt but impassive and unrelenting reality. Even a day's immersion in unadulterated being restores our souls.

For as a species we are constantly betrayed and betraying, deceiving even ourselves. We go about bleating in the most unabashed way, "Who am I?" The question would never occur to a carrot. Yet it seems the central occupation of human beings. We write plays, songs, and books reiterating the question and posing possible answers. We go to doctors, clinics, conferences, and church, holding the question in our mouths like a bolus we cannot quite swallow. Those who ignore or distract themselves from the question we call callous and loutish. But in the end our deception is inescapable. We cannot be true to a nature we know nothing of. We may be labeled *homo sapiens*, but the last thing we are likely to know is ourselves.

It is disagreeable to be such a cosmic embarrassment. Which is why it is a consolation to lie low and still and begin to match the thudding pulse to the emanations of the earth. I lift my lids very carefully and behold curves that move me, visual hooks that draw the very breath out of me without my understanding why. The reflexive curl of grama grass, the hill's horizon, arching limbs—the visual rhythms beat on my own vaulted rib cage. "Right" began by meaning a straight stick; "wrong" meant sour or twisted. And I would give my life to mean, once and purely, what a curl of grama grass says.

Merlin the magician once told Arthur that when a man lies, he kills a part of the world. Is this to be our final end, driving nature into the convergence of our consciousness, where we can murder it with our desperate falsehoods?

We are so clever in our embarrassing way. We can say both what we mean and what we don't mean and sometimes both together. We have a word, "technology," which is another name for predicting, which is another name for control, which is another name for distrust.

We were made the namers of this earth, and see what a job we have made of it. Connections between different bits of phenomena, such as a straight stick and our word "right," once seen as immediate reality echoing inside our own bell-bodies, are now only dismissed as metaphor—language technology, amusing tricks to decorate a meaning. But man, Emerson observed, "is an analogist, and studies relations in all objects." These analogies, the work of civilizations, are neither lucky nor capricious, he says, but "are constant and pervade nature." So we go on about our business, since in any case it is the only business we can undertake, doing it well or doing it poorly, making meaning or perverting it.

And at times one wonders about that logjam of unarticulated meaning, stressed and creaking all around us. Do mountainsides break off into avalanches with the unrelieved weight of it? Do volcanoes spew out their gastric juices in agonized aphasia? Do storms cry out for the psalm we should be singing? Do all the blood-drinking, bone-crunching beasts lift their heads in witless pain from their prey, snarling and spitting in the frustration of the futility to which they have been subjected, because they are dumb to name the true elements of their sacramental meal?

Would this be a eucharistic universe indeed if we would but speak the word? Could we elevate the admirable obedience of creation to coherent consciousness; would the morning stars sing together as they did when the cornerstone of creation was laid, before our terrible freedom descended like doom upon us? Would the hidden sea creatures, full of a barbarous beauty, echo from the salted depths, and the innards of earth heave themselves in roiling, molten music?

They are waiting—the mammoths metamorphosed into oil among the ferns, the ozone layer hovering like an eggshell over us, the alpine meadows sighing down mountainsides, the grizzlies and mosquitoes licking blood from their snouts—they are waiting to be sprung from their bondage to decay, to lift up and up and up their hearts.

They are waiting for us to get our act together. To find out the answer to our interminable question of who we are. The eggshell may collapse over our heads, all the hard-pressed mammoths and ferns be burnt in the great terrestrial funeral pyre, the mountains be leveled and beasts suck blood unsated. But they still must wait to be cured of corruption until we discover the answer to our riddle.

The revealing of the sons of God is what they wait for. They, poor futile creatures, know their own secrets, their own natures. It is we who are hidden from ourselves. It is we who await the revelation of our destiny.

"Man is the messiah of nature," Novalis wrote. A purblind, ignorant, contrary messiah. Dumb to his own destiny, he locks up the universe in futility, logjams the river of the water of life that flows through the new heaven and the new earth.

"There shall no more be anything accursed, but the throne of God and of the Lamb shall be in it, and his servants shall worship him." Not one quark but will be quick and no longer cursed. They will pour forth their very bodies in an ecstasy at holiness, at the completion of the consciousness of the cosmos. Then will the wind, now seen as only a spirit snagged in our little sails, be blessed as the breath of all being.

With his divine alchemy
He turns not only water into wine,
but common things into radiant mysteries,
yes, every meal into a eucharist,
and the jaws of the sepulchre
into an outgoing gate.

—George MacDonald

Chapter XII

So how many times have I set out for just that task? How
many miles have I covered in order to accompany a clump of
conifers? How many granite boulders have I honed myself on
like a nail dragged across emery?

I have tuned my sensory receptors to the Madison River in
Montana when its swollen surface turned to salmon's flesh in
a twilight saturated with moisture so that the colors caught
and held on a curtain of air and water. I have regarded
seabirds pushing off from the tip of Texas and launching
their improbable angles out over the grey Gulf. I have
stumbled on the tracks of a field mouse embroidered on the
snow where they emerged from a tiny tunnel, and have followed them to where they disappeared in a huge feathered
fan swept into the snow's surface by a bird's wings. And I
have given thanks for the mouse and thanks for the bird and
thanks for the tracks they left, like notes, scored on this vast
white sheet for the one who spies them out to sing.

For if you go poking about the world, intent on keeping
the candle of consciousness blazing, you must be ready to
give thanks at all times. Discrimination is not allowed. The
flame cannot gutter and fail when a cold wind whistles
through the house.

Thanksgiving, thanksgiving. All must be thanksgiving.

It took thirty-eight thousand Levites to give thanks to God
in David's day; every morning and every evening the shifts
changed. Four thousand were needed just to carry the hacked
carcasses of cattle, and another four thousand were needed to
sing about it. The place reeked of blood, was soaked in
blood. The priests stood around gnawing and chewing and
giving thanks. They did not cross-stitch their gratitude on
samplers to frame and hang on the wall. They wrote their
thanks in blood on the doorposts every year.

Thanksgiving is not a task to be undertaken lightly. It is not for dilettantes or aesthetes. One does not dabble in praise for one's own amusement, nor train the intellect and develop perceptual skills in order to add to his repertoire. We're not talking about the world as a free course in art appreciation. No. Thanksgiving is not a *result* of perception; thanksgiving is the *access* to perception. Or, as Laurel Lee wrote, some things have to be believed to be seen. Only the open heart, the open eye, the open throat can take in the world.

Thanksgiving is a hard task, not an easy sentiment. If it weren't, it would hardly be a proper human activity. It may be natural for the heavens to declare the glory of God, but thanksgiving must be wrung from the throats of those who necessarily weigh, analyze, make distinctions. It is all one to the heavens, whether they are sodden with moisture lifted from the waters below or whether they burn like scorched copper over a barren desert. Each has its own beauty, its own inner consistency to maintain. But it is not all one to us. We are terrified by the knowledge of our own lack of necessity to the universe.

This is why we can have a little pity for Pietro Bernardone, the father of Saint Francis. "It is not me who no longer needs God," he told his bishop. "It is God who does not need me, apparently. He acts for his own self-interest, and, as you see, I don't seem to fit into that scheme." It is hard to give thanks when one gives up one's child. Perhaps that is why thanksgiving was sealed in blood by the Hebrews. They remember Abraham climbing the hill in Moriah with Isaac, the fire and the knife in his hand.

And the saint of Assisi himself pushed the possibility of praise to its limits. It is easy to imagine Francis on a Zefferelli screen, giving thanks while gamboling on a green hillside bejeweled with blossoms. But when he had driven nature into a corner, he found it filled not just with birds and flowers but with starving wolves and howling winter winds and leprous pus. How did he manage to bleat out his thin little hymn then?

Other holy men of a less vehement constitution have

sought oblivion, relief for and obliteration of the senses, a dissolution of the scalded, scarred consciousness. The disjunction between desire and fulfillment is too bitter. And it is
precisely by perception that we are betrayed into desire, an
unslakeable thirst for that which deceives us by dying. The
truth that Augustine cried out for from the marrow of his
soul lies ultimately in no thing, such wisdom warns. Therefore, eschew the bird, the bloom, the bosom of the beloved.
Such things do not last. They are corruptible. They are illusion. Only the uncreated lasts.

But how does one go chasing after a glimpse of the uncreated Light? The Hesychasts, high on Mount Athos, bowed
their heads upon their breasts, took a deep breath, and
plunged in. What they plunged into was prayer. It began
with a tack with which to fix the attention. It became breath
itself, an inlet for the universe to invade one's body until the
entire cosmos, drawn in, heaved out, was transformed into
prayer. The body's posture was important. The breathing was
to be carefully controlled so as to keep time with the words.
Eventually the prayer, breathed in, united with their very
blood and heartbeat; breathed out, it blessed the world. And
some monks claimed after a while to have indeed seen the
Light of the Transfiguration, uncreated energy beheld by
bodily eyes.

Their Western brothers attacked both the physical method
of the Hesychasts' prayer and their claim that the Beatific Vision could be sensually perceived as phenomenon. It was only
God's essence that could be apprehended by such as Moses
and Paul. Small matter that Moses, at any rate, would have
had no notion of what an essence was. He was satisfied with
burning bushes and a glimpse of God's back. And the light
that Paul saw was phenomenal enough to have blinded him.
The opponents of the Hesychasts might as well have been
Buddhists for all their attempts to transcend what they
were—their bodies.

For it is bodies that are baptized, bodies that eat and absorb the Body of Christ, bodies that will be raised, glorified
and incorruptible. It is tongues that confess and knees that

bow. Perhaps we are so willing to reduce ourselves to abstractions of thought, principles of personality, because God, too, could then be an abstraction or a principle, and not a person.

How dare we say we feed Christ in the hungry, harbor him in the stranger, succor him in the sick, if we believe the Incarnation is over and done with? God save us from perverting metaphors to moralizing. Is "Christ in us" only sentiment? Is time stronger than eternity, and has it kicked God himself back upstairs into his properly ethereal realm? Do we gloat over our own transience and our decaying corpses, thinking that can hold him at bay?

He is here, rushing in our blood, melting in our mouths, oscillating in our synapses. In him all things hold together. He pierces us with photons, skewering us like Tinker Toys to all creation. When we lift up our hearts we must also lift up, on that slender pinnacle of purpose, the whole world. We carry mountains on our tongue. Bless the Lord, O my soul, we say, and all that is within me. And within us is the Sahara, the salty seas, the muddy Mississippi. The flora and fauna of the equator swarm our throats. Asphalt and ashes. The cedar tree. The pond. All the world that we have discovered, one way or another. That is what is within us and what must be made to bless the Lord.

Christ lies spread-eagled across our map, like the map of the Ebsdorf monks, holding everything together. He grows underground, undergirding the soil itself like the thin white threads of nitrogen-fixing bacteria. He sucks and blows the stars, in and out, imploding, exploding. He instructs waves about their functions and buries knowledge in the heart of each photon. Through him and for him this happens. Creation is a birthday gift for the Son. The birth is eternal, never-ending; thus the gift itself is upheld by the eternity of the occasion.

All the world is one great sacramental loaf. We are not— nor will we ever be, God save us—solitary intelligences spinning in the dark void of space. He crowds upon us from Sheol to the sea; he jostles our thoughts along the pathways in our brains. He hides in the bushes, jumping out in flames to startle us into seeing. He sequesters himself in stables and swaddling so as to take us unawares. He veils himself in flesh, the same flesh that drips into fingers at the end of my arms and sprouts into hair on my head.

Either the world is holy or it's not. Either the creator's work is a sign of himself or it's a sham. Where else can one draw the line between sacred and profane except around all the cosmos? For "profane" meant, originally, outside the temple, and all creation was, in the beginning, a temple for God's "very good." Whenever we eat, drink, breathe, see, take anything in by any means, we are commanded to remember the sacrifice. We try to hedge in the holy, to pour it into tiny, trivial cups, to make the bread as pale and tasteless as possible, like fingernails. We are saying to God: Get away from me. Just so the desert Israelites implored Moses to keep God on the mountain and not bring him down among their tents. As though our immolation by the holy were not our only hope.

Still, we take the big black crayon in our hands and draw these little islands where we will let God live in the world. In the tiny cups and on the unfamiliar silver plates so cold you can see your breath on them. We cover him up with white linen napkins just as they did in the grave. We draw more lines around Bibles and sanctuaries, thus adding a few more islands to this archipelago of the holy, and there you have it. Little concentration camps for Christ. Our incremental piety bristles around the perimeters like barbed wire, hemming him in.

I stumbled upon an outdoor chapel in the mountains one day. It was midmorning, and the wind was still gentle. The sun's rays were extraordinarily straight and undeflected in that high, clear air. I sat down on a log laid lengthwise that made the back pew. It was still early spring in the mountains, and the new warmth released the winter-long scents pent up in the earth around me. The cross, two pine posts nailed at right angles and shored up by stones, stood across from me, outlined by the graduated blues of a lake below and the sky above.

I happened to notice, my eye caught by the movement, a glistening black wasp, not much bigger than a housefly, dragging a bloated, brownish-red spider across the sand beside my pew. When it got to a small hole in the sand it stopped, stuck its head inside the hole, and dug it out a bit more, enlarging the entrance and piling up a minute mound of backfill at the hole's mouth. Then it hurried back to the spider, who for all I know might have been only temporarily anesthetized, and dragging the cumbersome body behind it, disappeared down the hole.

At about the same time an ant wandered by, smelled spider, and did what it was obviously programmed to do. It grabbed one of the spider's legs that was still filling the entrance to the hole and started tugging. The elasticity of the leg amazed me; it stretched out quite like a thin rubber band in the ant's grasp. Meanwhile, below, the wasp was dragging the spider ever downward. The ant shifted its grip several times in the struggle. But weight, the angle of descent, and gravity were all on the wasp's side. The spider finally disappeared completely down the hole, where the wasp no doubt laid eggs and attached them to the spider's body so that there would be fresh meat for the larvae when they hatched. For a while the ant ran around distractedly in ever widening circles, wringing its antennae, until it forgot the scent and set a staggering course across the sand again.

I sat there for a good while longer, looking at other things, watching a boat of trollers out in the lake. Then the cross, silver-grey and outspread across the blue, said something: This is my body.

I glanced sharply at the wasp hole in the sand again. All was still. Below, the wasp was probably busy with the stupefied spider. The ant was somewhere stumbling through a world made of food and not-food.

This is my body, given for you.

Who was it talking to? Me or the wasp?

The cross, fibered and fierce, thrust itself into the hillside and out into the lake and sky. This is my body.

Given for the futility in which wasp, spider, and ant also struggle? Chapels may be natural enough places for wasps and spiders and ants to invade. But what happens when sacrifice invades the world? When crosses are found, unexpectedly, on rock hillsides?

Life without sacrifice, Annie Dillard wrote, is an abomination. Never to give oneself up, always to hoard and protect. Without heat constantly being given up and taken in, this world would grind to a halt of absolute zero temperature. There would be no more being, which after all depends on the continual exchange of energy to maintain its existence. Elementary particles must suffer a continual state of dissolution and regrouping. Trees, in order to live, must suck up the soil and exhale the air. Our jellied corpses melt into meadow rue. All dying does somebody good. The meanest miser must unclench his fist and unfold it, one day, in a flower, even if that is the only graceful gesture he ever makes.

The heart of the universe is sacrifice, not the stone-cold nirvana of oblivion. To live in Christ we must die to ourselves, be careless of our own substance.

Suffering is the sole origin of consciousness, Dostoyevsky claimed. And those of us who would grow into the consciousness of Christ—is this not also our part to speak? This is my body, given for you? Do we not, as Paul insisted, complete in our bodies the sufferings of Christ? Do we not, Christ in us, continue the Incarnation?

Dostoyevsky's continual prayer was that he might be equal to his sufferings. For what else can we equal, and, falling short of that sum, what diminished definition can we claim? That of a spider, a wasp, an ant, eating and eaten, but with no words of thanksgiving, no knowledge of our necessity.

We can never transcend our mute mouths, never vault upward into the air and know ourselves to be, incredibly, flying, until we are willing to suffer our small—and great— deaths. Until we enter into the sacrifice at the center of the world, that fulcrum on which all being is balanced, all our thanksgiving is nothing but a sigh of relief at one more day's reprieve. How can we ever become more than we are but by dying?

Then we crack the world. Creation ceases to groan and lifts up its head and looks around. Echoing down all the intertwined wave frequencies comes the memory of creation. Even the ant, raised to more reality, knows more than food and not-food, and the spider will perhaps, one day, gladly give himself to the wasp and her children. The earth, the universe, the cosmos will consciously be what it now dumbly is—a continual outpouring, a perpetual torrent of being saying, this is my body. A eucharistic universe transmuting energy into matter and sacrifice into substance.

How else can creation be completed except by consciousness, by singing its being, manifesting its self, through the sacrifice of thanksgiving!

But how many billion years will such a task take? How many eager sacrifices are undertaken each day? How many crosses borne, deaths died? Enough to enhance one slug's apprehension of its creator? Enough to shake the futility from a single sloth? How many stones could cry out from our emulation of our own savior?

I sit in yet another coffee shop, watching the sky caught between the morning's melting snow showers and the afternoon's rinsing clear of clouds. Just as much I am watching the people, doing my God-spying, preparing a place for the ingress of the Spirit. I am looking, as John did, for the life made manifest, the matter in which the Spirit is pleased to dwell.

The spy must watch with all his care and attention in order to catch this gusty God who blows where he will. He must train himself to see Christ in the faces passing by—to look at them with that specific intent, whetted to a needle's sharp point. Because if we can ever attempt the discipline of seeing Christ there, we in a sense create him there, call him into the world. Just as we create the goodness of gifts by knowing—acknowledging—them as gifts, and good. Otherwise the gifts fall to the ground, impotent to do us good. We stuff straw in our mouths, not knowing it to be God.

"Jesus could not do miracles where unbelief hindered," Blake pointed out; "hence we must conclude that the man who holds miracles to be ceased puts it out of his own power to ever witness one." Jesus had to be believed in order to be efficacious. And today he still must be believed in by us, by our seeing his face in those streaming past us.

This is not sentiment or morality. This is consciousness catching hold of phenomena. When it is done we see miracles—we see the kingdom itself, the life made manifest.

Some faces one sees have shadows on them; ruts of unbeing are scored along the mouth and eyes. It hurts to look at them, those faces that have chosen their own decarnation and destruction. But so far as any face continues to exist, it does so by the upholding power of its creator. There is no face, then, that is not incarnated, however much of its meaning it may have allowed to slip into chaos.

All dust, whatever shape it takes—motes, molecules, men—is holy, sacramental, participates in the Incarnation. We testify to this, if only tacitly, each time we recoil from scars of every kind on the earth's face. We draw back from slag heaps and seal slaughters and other such unmakings because they too are a desecration of the Incarnation. Those who have the power to see Christ in lepers are also those who call the sun and moon their brother and sister.

This world is holy, having come from a holy hand. Why did we ever separate it into sacred and secular? Was it so that we would have a place to feel safe from holiness?

But Christ invades us even so. All we have to do is open our eyes. True, opening the eyes is very difficult. One might as well command a stone to shout—it requires that kind of concentration. But in the end, that's all there is, this God-spying. Either you open your eyes and see, or there's nothing there. Not the world, not you, nothing.

I look around at the people gathered unwittingly with me for this sacrament at Sambo's. A couple of postmen who came in from the cold are warming themselves over their coffee. A businessman in baggy polyester makes bad jokes for the benefit of the thin waitress. I think a mountain might be easier to move, to lift up, than the man at the end of the counter slumped on his stool in spider-like torpor. In the booth next to mine is a lady in yellow-grey coronet braids, and behind her a cowboy with his girlfriend and weekend-custody baby. There is nothing very remarkable about any of us except the image of God shining from and sunk into our faces, the mark of which, according to Hasidic legend, even the demons beg to be allowed to behold.

Perhaps these strangers (at whom I am stealing glances as avidly as any demon) don't know, any more than the wasp, that a sacrifice at the center of the world upholds their life. Perhaps they don't know that their hands are holy and are holding holy things. Perhaps they are unaware that they are dripping grace into their mouths and masticating their salvation. To them it's only French fries and catsup, coffee and doughnuts, only light and clatter, if that much. The wonder of the world is invading their bodies, while being itself—transfigured into thought, perception, praise, motion—evades them.

But for me, for a moment at least, there is an extraordinary sweetness in these faces. The light breaks across them, they lift and turn, call to one another. They are a long way from unbeing and diminishment. Even should they not know and bless the Life that is in them or confess whose it is, it knows and blesses them. It winks at me slyly from their unsuspecting faces, bounds outside to the last shred of cloud, and slouches past the window again, disguised as the indifferent afternoon paperboy.

Bibliography

Barfield, Owen. *Saving the Appearances.* New York: Harcourt Brace Jovanovich, 1965.

Bell, J. S., and M. Naunnberg. "Moral Aspects of Quantum Mechanics." In *Preludes in Theoretical Physics in Honor of V. F. Weisskopf.* Amsterdam: North-Holland Publishing Co., 1966.

Bohm, David. *The Special Theory of Relativity.* Menlo Park, California: Benjamin-Cummings, 1965.

——. *Wholeness and the Implicate Order.* Boston: Routledge & Kegan Paul, 1980.

Capra, Fritjof. *The Tao of Physics.* Boulder, Colorado: Shambhala Publications, 1975.

Dillard, Annie. *Holy the Firm.* New York: Bantam Books, 1979.

Greider, Ken. *Invitation to Physics.* New York: Harcourt Brace Jovanovich, 1973.

Heisenberg, Werner. *Physics and Beyond.* New York: Harper & Row, 1971.

Judson, Horace Freeland. *The Search for Solutions.* Holt, Rinehart & Winston, 1980.

MacKay, Donald M. *Brains, Machines, and Persons.* Grand Rapids: Eerdmans, 1980.

Morrison, Philip. "Time's Arrow and External Perturbations." In *Preludes in Theoretical Physics in Honor of V. F. Weisskopf* (see above).

Regush, Nicholas, and June Regush. *The New Consciousness Catalog.* New York: G. P. Putnam's Sons, 1979.

Toulmin, Stephen, ed. *Quanta and Reality.* American Research Council, 1962.

Wolf, Fred A. *Taking the Quantum Leap: The New Physics for the Nonscientist.* New York: Harper & Row, 1981.

Zukav, Gary. *The Dancing Wu Li Masters: An Overview of the New Physics.* New York: Wm. Morrow, 1979.